# Holt MUSIC

**Eunice Boardman Meske**
Professor of Music and Education
University of Wisconsin—Madison
Madison, Wisconsin

**Mary P. Pautz**
Assistant Professor of Music
  Education
University of Wisconsin—Milwaukee
Milwaukee, Wisconsin

**Barbara Andress**
Professor of Music Education
Arizona State University
Tempe, Arizona

**Fred Willman**
Professor of Music and Education
University of Missouri—St. Louis
St. Louis, Missouri

**Holt, Rinehart and Winston, Publishers**
**New York, Toronto, Mexico City, London, Sydney, Tokyo**

## Special Consultants

Nancy Archer
Forest Park Elementary School
Fort Wayne, Indiana

Joan Z. Fyfe
Jericho Public Schools
Jericho, New York

Jeanne Hook
Albuquerque Public Schools
Albuquerque, New Mexico

Danette Littleton
University of Tennessee at Chattanooga
Chattanooga, Tennessee

Barbara Reeder Lundquist
University of Washington
Seattle, Washington

Ollie McFarland
Detroit Public Schools
Detroit, Michigan

Faith Norwood
Harnett County School District
North Carolina

Linda K. Price
Richardson Independent School District
Richardson, Texas

Dawn L. Reynolds
District of Columbia Public Schools
Washington, D.C.

Morris Stevens
A.N. McCallum High School
Austin, Texas

Jack Noble White
Texas Boys Choir
Fort Worth, Texas

ISBN 0-03-005309-9
890 041 9876543

Acknowledgements for previously copyrighted material and credits for photographs and art start on page 253.

# Table of Contents

CORE

# Unit 1

# Music To Explore

# *The First Quarter*

## I Got Rhythm

Words by Ira Gershwin                                    Music by George Gershwin

1. I ___ got       rhy - thm, __       I ___ got       mu - sic, __
2. I ___ got       dais - ies __       in ___ green     pas - tures, __

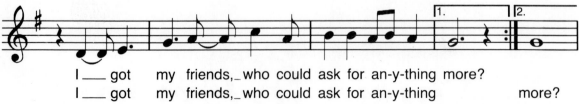

I ___ got       my friends, __ who could ask for an-y-thing more?
I ___ got       my friends, __ who could ask for an-y-thing       more?

6

Old __ Man    Trou - ble, __        I __ don't    mind    him. __

You __    won't    find    him __        'Round __    my        door.

I __    got        star - light, __        I __    got        sweet    dreams, __

I __    got        my        friends, __ who could ask for an - y-thing    more,

Who could    ask        for        an - y - thing        more?

**LISTENING**

# Porgy and Bess

Overture

by George Gershwin

LISTEN TO THE SYNCOPATED RHYTHMS

# Closer to Your Love

by Al Jarreau, Tom Canning, and Jay Graydon

Count 1–2–3–4–5–6–7–8.

Perform one hand jive action to each count.

1 ♩ ♩  pat knees

2 ♩ ♩  clap hands

3 ♩ ♩  right over left hand

4 ♩ ♩  left over right hand

5 ♩ ♩  right fist tap on left fist

6 ♩ ♩  left fist tap on right fist

7 ♩ ♩  "hitchhike" with right thumb over right shoulder

8 ♩ ♩  "hitchhike" with left thumb over left shoulder

Perform the hand jive while listening to the music. Follow the circled numbers.

Introduction

┌─ Get ready ─┐        ┌──── Begin hand jive ────────┐
⑧  ⑧  —  ⑧ ⑧ ⑧    ⑧ ⑧ ⑧
(pattern set)        (vocalist enters . . . sings Verse 1)

┌─ Continue ──────────────────────────────┐
⑧ ⑧    ⑧ ⑧ ⑧ ⑧    ⑧ ⑧ ⑧ ⑧
(Refrain)    (Verse 2)        (Refrain)

┌─ Rest ─┐  ┌ Solo 1 ┐  ┌ Solo 2 ┐  ┌─ All hand jive ─┐
⑧ ⑧    ⑧ ⑧    ⑧  ⑧    ⑧ ⑧ ⑧ ⑧
(instruments,  (Refrain)        (fade out . . .) Bend lower
then voice)                      and lower to
                                 the ground

# Rag Mop

Words and Music by Johnnie Lee Wills and Deacon Anderson

Tap the short sounds on your leg or a cymbal. Chant the rhythm of the melody as it flows in relation to these short sounds. Don't get "caught" speaking on the rests!

# Add a Rhythm

Can you add?

$$1 + 1 = ?$$
$$2 + 2 = ?$$
$$4 + 4 = ?$$

Then you can do musical addition!  ⌣ = +

Learn the rhythm of a new song by
adding the short sounds together.
Begin with a series of short sounds.
Tap a pencil eraser on the desk
or lightly tap with your fingertips.

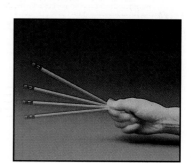

Now perform the rhythm of the song in
relation to this series of short sounds.

♩ tells you to **rest** even though the short pulse continues.
Remember to follow the musical plus signs!
Add two or more sounds together.

Rid - ing a - long and sing - ing   my   bi - cy - cle   song, _____

Float - ing with   no care like   a       bird __ on   the     air; _____

Glid - ing with   ease and weav - ing   gent - ly through the   trees; _____

Bi - cy - cling   is such mel - low   fun,     so         let's go!

10

# The Bicycle Song

Words and Music by Jack Noble White

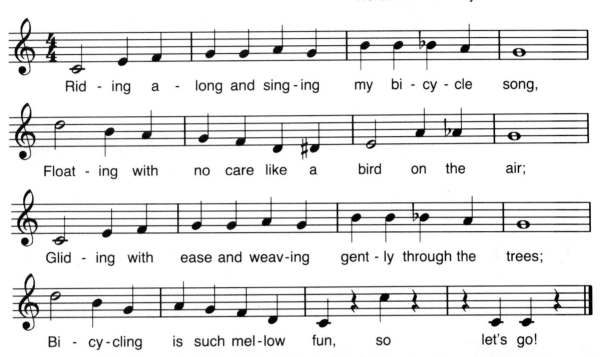

Rid - ing a - long and sing - ing my bi - cy - cle song,

Float - ing with no care like a bird on the air;

Glid - ing with ease and weav - ing gent - ly through the trees;

Bi - cy - cling is such mel - low fun, so let's go!

# The Motor Car

Words and Music by Jack Noble White

Sing this tune as a partner song
with "The Bicycle Song."

1. Won't you come and take a ride with me a-round the town in
2. See the peo - ple wav - ing mer - ri - ly as we pass by and

my new fan - cy mo - tor car, bump - ing up and down.
honk our clas - sy lit - tle horn. Watch for that cow in the road!

Hear the mo - tor chug - ging "Put - ty, put - ty, putt."
I'm not sure just where we

Is - n't this great? Real - ly first rate? You get the gate.

Let's take a look down this road.
are. Watch that pud - dle there.

Oh, no! Shucks! We're stuck!

# Twelfth-Street Rag

by Euclay Bowman and Andy Razaf

Add short sounds to create the rhythm of the melody. Tap each short sound. Make long or short sounds of rhythm by saying "Ch" or "Ch——."

*Theme I*
*(Repeat 3 times)*

ch   ch

*(Rest 2 measures; sense the shorter sounds.)*

*(Repeat 2 times)*

# Meet Me in St. Louis, Louis

Words by Andrew Sterling

Music by Kerry Mills

How long is each musical idea?
How many smaller parts does each idea contain?
Which ideas are the same? almost the same?

Meet me in St. Lou - is, Lou - is,

Meet me at the fair; _____

Don't tell me the lights are shin - ing

An - y place but there. _____

We will dance the Hooch - ee Kooch - ee, _____

I will be your toot - sie woot - sie; _____

Meet me in St. Lou - is, Lou - is,

Meet me at the fair. _____

Add this accompaniment:
bells or bass xylophone

# Seventy-Six Trombones

from *The Music Man*

Words and Music by Meredith Willson

Sev-en-ty - six trom - bones led the big pa - rade,____

With a hun-dred and ten cor - nets close at hand.____

They were fol-lowed by rows and rows of the fin-est vir-tu - o - sos,

The cream of ev - ery fa - mous band.____

Sev-en-ty - six trom - bones caught the morn-ing sun.____

With a hun-dred and ten cor - nets close be - hind.____

16

There were more than a thou-sand reeds spring-ing up like weeds,

There were horns __ of ev - ery shape and kind. _____

There were cop - per bot - tom tym - pa - ni in horse pla-toons, ____

Thun - der-ing, thun - der-ing all a-long the way.

Dou - ble bell eu - pho - ni-ums and big bas - soons, ____

Each bas - soon _____ hav - ing his big fat say.

There were fif - ty mount-ed can-nons in the bat - ter-y, _____

Thun-der-ing, thun-der-ing loud-er than be-fore.

Clar-i-nets of ev-ery size and trum-pet-ers who'd im-pro-vise

A full oc-tave high-er than the score.

Sev-en-ty - six trom - bones led the big pa - rade,_____

When the or-der to march rang out loud and clear._____

Start-ing off with a big bong bong on a Chi-nese gong

By a big bong bong-er at the rear._____

Sev-en-ty - six trom - bones hit the coun-ter-point,_____

While a hun-dred and ten cor - nets played the air. _____

Then I mod-est-ly took my place as the one and on - ly bass,

And I oom - pahed up and down the square. _____

# Goodnight, My Someone

from *The Music Man*

Words and Music
by Meredith Willson

Goodnight, my someone, goodnight, my love.
Sleep tight, my someone, sleep tight, my love.

Our star is shining its brightest light,
For goodnight, my love, for goodnight.

Sweet dreams be yours, dear, if dreams there be;
Sweet dreams to carry you close to me.

I wish they may, and I wish they might,
Now goodnight, my someone, goodnight.

# Midnight

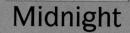

Words and Music by Robert Starer

**Gently moving**

It is mid-night; it is mid-night.

The sun is shin - ing bright - ly

And a car is rac - ing slow - ly down the riv - er.

It is sum-mer; it is sum-mer.

Snow is fall - ing light - ly.

It is warm and yet I shiv - er.

I saw a rock - et walk._ I heard a tur - tle talk. _

I saw a dog with three legs. I saw four square eggs.

Do you    know, do you know why I    shiv - er?

It    is    mid-night;        it    is    mid-night.

The        sun    is    shin - ing        bright - ly

And    a    car    is    rac - ing        slow - ly down the    riv - er.

It    is    hot,        ver - y    hot.        It    is

ver - y,    ver - y    hot and yet    I    shiv - er.

## LISTENING

# Little Fugue in G Minor

### by Johann Sebastian Bach

The composer of "Midnight" used one important melody several times. J. S. Bach also used one important melody several times in this piece, which is called a **fugue**. How many times can you hear this melody, which is called the **subject**?

# Hallelujah Chorus

## from *Messiah*

by Georg Friedrich Handel

Hallelujah! Hallelujah!
For the Lord God Omnipotent reigneth.
The kingdom of this world is become
The Kingdom of our Lord and of His Christ;
And He shall reign forever and ever.
King of Kings and Lord of Lords.

This selection for chorus is four minutes long. It contains only the words given above. Will you be able to learn this song just by listening to it?

As you listen, follow this "musical map." Listen for call numbers.

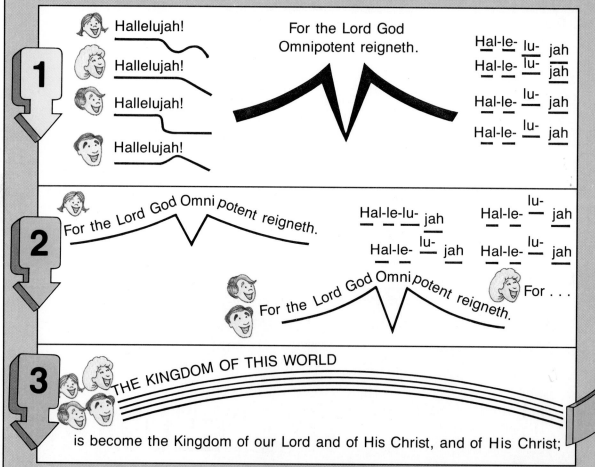

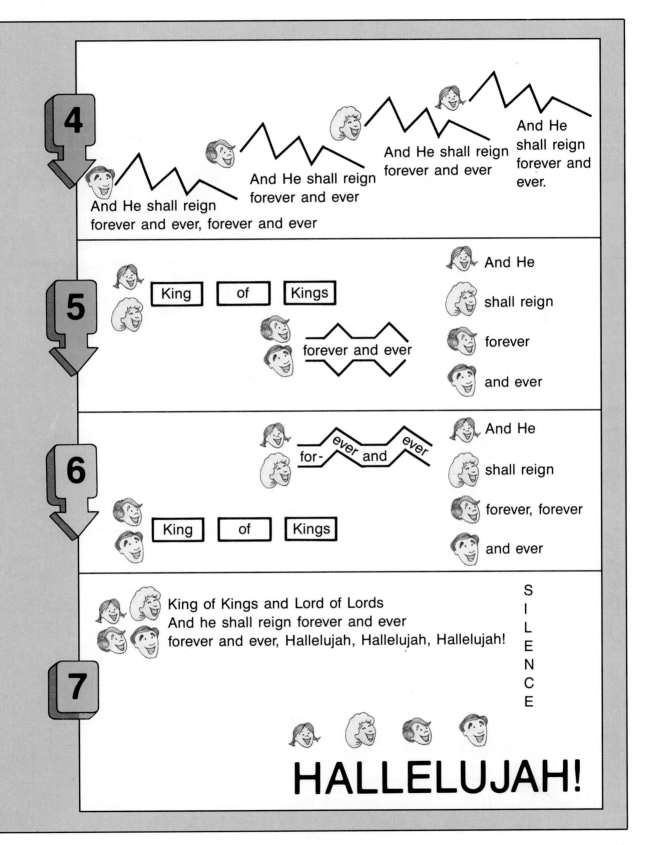

**4**

And He shall reign forever and ever, forever and ever

And He shall reign forever and ever

And He shall reign forever and ever

And He shall reign forever and ever.

**5**

King of Kings

forever and ever

And He shall reign forever and ever

**6**

for-ever and ever

King of Kings

And He shall reign forever, forever and ever

**7**

King of Kings and Lord of Lords
And he shall reign forever and ever
forever and ever, Hallelujah, Hallelujah, Hallelujah!

SILENCE

HALLELUJAH!

When someone speaks to you, what do you hear?

sounds?          words?          ideas?          feelings?

What makes the difference?

**pitch?**          rhythm?          **accents?**          volume?          **articulation?**

What do you hear when someone sings?

words?          melody?          rhythm?          dynamics?          articulation?

## The Power and Glory

Words and Music by Phil Ochs

1. & 4. C'-mon and    take a walk with  me through this green and grow-in'    land,
    2. ⅞ From __    Col - o - ra -do, Kan-sas, and the  Car - o - li - nas,  too, Vir -
    3. ⅞ Yet she's  on -  ly  as  rich   as   the  poor -est  of the    poor,

Walk through the    mead-ows and the    moun-tains  and the    sand,
gin - ia   and   A - las - ka,  from the    old __   to the    new,
On - ly     as    free __   as   a    pad -locked pris-on    door,

24

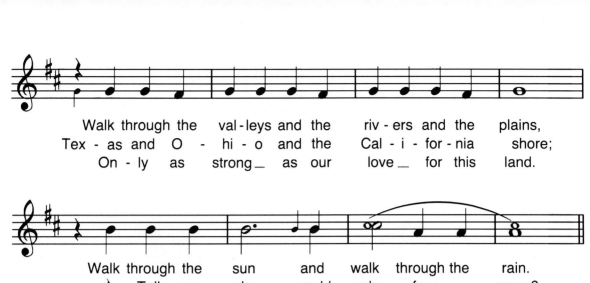

Walk through the val-leys and the riv-ers and the plains,
Tex - as and O - hi - o and the Cal - i - for - nia shore;
On - ly as strong _ as our love _ for this land.

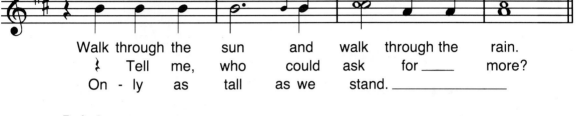

Walk through the sun and walk through the rain.
Tell me, who could ask for ___ more?
On - ly as tall as we stand. ___

*Refrain*

Here's a land full of pow - er and glo - ry,

Beau - ty that words can-not re - call. ___

Oh, her pow - er shall rest on the strength of her free-dom,

Her glo - ry shall rest on us all. ___

___ On us all, on us all. ___

# Gonna Build a Mountain

### Words and Music by Leslie Bricusse and Anthony Newley

How will you use tempo, **dynamics,** and articulation to express
the ideas of this song?

Gon-na build a moun-tain___Yeah, yeah

From a lit-tle     hill.     Yeah, yeah

Gon-na build a  moun-tain___Yeah, yeah

Least I hope I      will.   Yeah, yeah

Gon-na build a  moun-tain___Yeah, yeah

Gon-na build it     high.  Yeah, yeah

I don't know how I'm gon-na do it,   on-ly know I'm gon-na  try. Yeah, yeah

## LISTENING

# Symphonie Fantastique
### Fourth Movement
by Hector Berlioz

Listen to this composition.

| | |
|---|---|
| **The First Time:** | Think about the mood suggested. |
| **The Second Time:** | Follow a "musical map." Notice the character of each melody. How does the character of each melody help shape the mood? |
| **The Third Time:** | How do other elements help to express the story? |

The title of this **movement** is "March to the Scaffold." Each movement of this symphony tells part of a story. Here is the composer's description of this part.

*The artist dreams that he has killed his beloved. He dreams that he is condemned and led to the scaffold, and that he is witnessing his own execution. The procession moves forward to the sounds of a march that is now somber and fierce, now brilliant and solemn, in which the muffled noise of heavy steps gives way to the noisiest clamor. At the end of the march, the first four measures of the beloved's theme appear, like a last thought of love, interrupted by the fatal blow.*

Listen again. How do the themes help "tell the story"? What other musical elements contribute to the mood of this music?

# Me and My Captain

Traditional

**The First Time:**

Everyone sit in a circle.

Person 1:    Play a G minor **chord** on the autoharp.
                Strum it over and over.

Person 2:    "Pull" a sound from the many you hear.
                Sing it on "loo."
                Sustain it as long as you wish.
                Then tap your neighbor on the shoulder.

Person 3:    Find a different sound in the autoharp chord.
                Sing it.

**The Second Time:**

Begin as before. This time, when the person signals a neighbor, he or she should take a breath and continue to sing. Listen to the sound of the vocal chord that results.

**The Third Time:**

After half of the circle has joined into the chord, the remainder of the circle should sing "Me and My Captain." Most of the melody uses the tones of the chord you've been singing.

1. Me and my cap - tain don't a - gree,
2. Got one mind for the cap - tain to see,
3. One of these days and it won't be long,

But he don't know 'cause he don't know me.
An - oth - er for what I know is me.
He'll call my name but I'll be gone.

*Refrain*

He don't know, he don't know my mind, when he sees me laugh-in',

Just laugh-in' to keep from cry - in'. _____

## Sometimes I Feel Like a Motherless Child

American Folk Song

Engage in your second "pulling sounds" activity again. Choose, then sustain, the sounds of the chord you hear. This time the person playing the autoharp will change chords. You will need to listen carefully to be ready to find a sound that fits when the second chord is heard.

After you've practiced going back and forth between the chords, some people should sing the following melody while others continue the vocal chording accompaniment. The chord symbols above the staff will tell you when to change.

Some-times I feel like a moth-er-less child, ___

Some-times I feel like a moth-er-less child, ___

Some-times I feel like a moth-er-less child, ___

A long way ___ from home, ___

A long way ___ from home. ___

# All Night Long

Traditional Black American Song

1. All night long, _____ all night long, _____
All night long, _____ from mid-night on.
Down by the sta-tion _____ read-y to go, _____
If the train don't come, _____ some-thing's wrong down the road.

2. If anyone asks you who wrote this song,
   Tell 'em I did – I sing it all night long.
   All night long, all night long,
   Tell 'em I did – I sing it all night long.

30

Harmonize "All Night Long."

You can add a harmony part by ear.
Can you add a harmony part by following this graph?

**First Time**

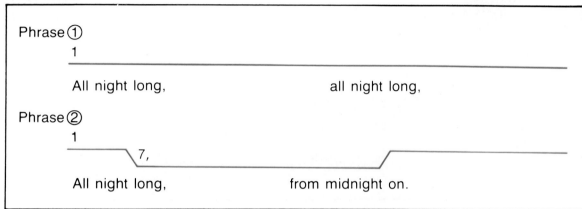

Phrase ①

All night long,                    all night long,

Phrase ②

All night long,                    from midnight on.

**Second Time**

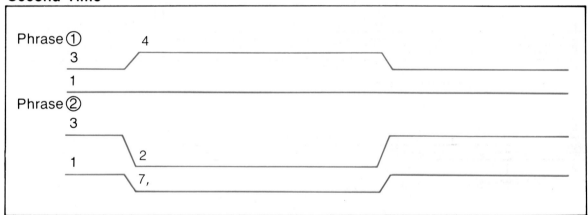

**Third Time**

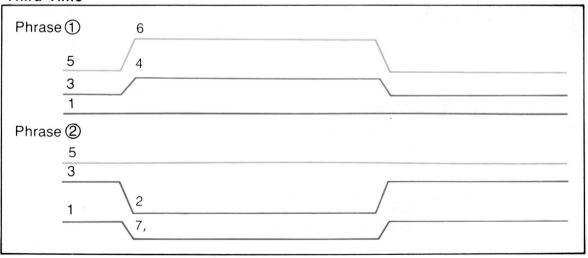

# The Marching Band

Different band directors use different combinations of instruments. This is the instrumentation of the band at one of the "Big Ten" midwestern universities.

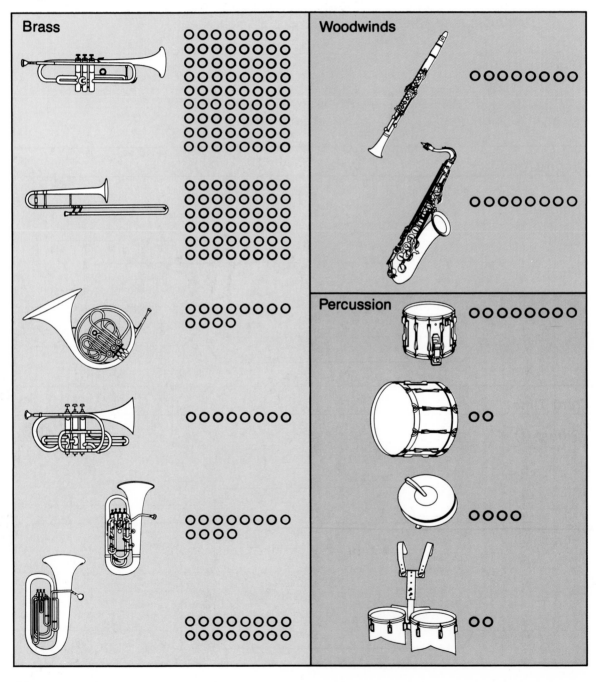

# The Symphonic Band

Here is the instrumentation for a typical symphonic band. It might vary depending on the composition being played. Each dot stands for one instrument. Compare this instrumentation with that of the marching band on page 32.

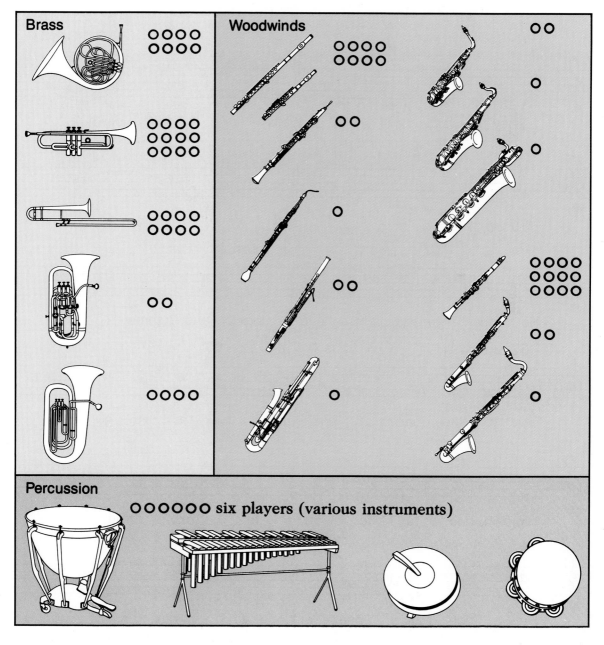

**Brass**

**Woodwinds**

**Percussion**

OOOOOO six players (various instruments)

# Mister Touchdown, U.S.A.

Words and Music by Ruth Roberts, Gene Piller, and William Katz

Play this rhythm on a snare drum.

They al - ways call him Mis - ter Touch - down. ____

They al - ways call him Mis - ter Team. ____

He can run ____ and kick and throw. ____

Give him the ball ____ and just look at him go. ____

Hip, hip, hoo - ray for Mis - ter Touch - down. ____

He's gon - na beat 'em to - day. ____

34

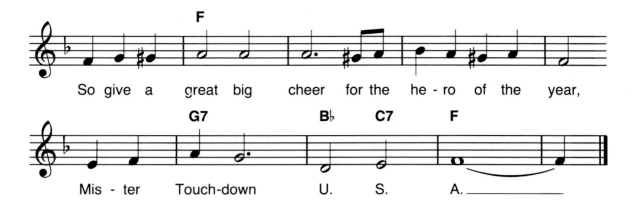

So give a great big cheer for the he - ro of the year,

Mis - ter Touch-down U. S. A. _____

## LISTENING

# On Wisconsin

### by Carl Beck and W. T. Purdy

Listen to a marching band perform "On Wisconsin." Compare it to an arrangement performed by a symphonic band. What differences do you notice?

# The Liberty Bell March

by John Philip Sousa

The march has always been a favorite musical form of American audiences, whether performed by a marching or a symphonic band. Listen to this march composed by John Philip Sousa, the "March King" of America. It is played by a symphonic band.

The first eight measures of each main theme are given here. Follow the notation as you listen. How often does each theme return? In what order do they occur?

# *Review 1*

## Jemmy Taylor-O

Words and Music by Jean Ritchie

**Brightly**

*Verse*

1. Jem - my Tay - lor - O goes down - town,
2. Jem - my Tay - lor - O go-in' down the road,

All the pret - ty girls ___ fol - ler him a - round.
Sing - in' like a bull - frog and hop - pin' like a toad.

*Chorus*

Heigh-O - did-dle-i - day. ___ Heigh-ho, did-dle-i-day,

And a heigh - ho, did - dle - i - day.

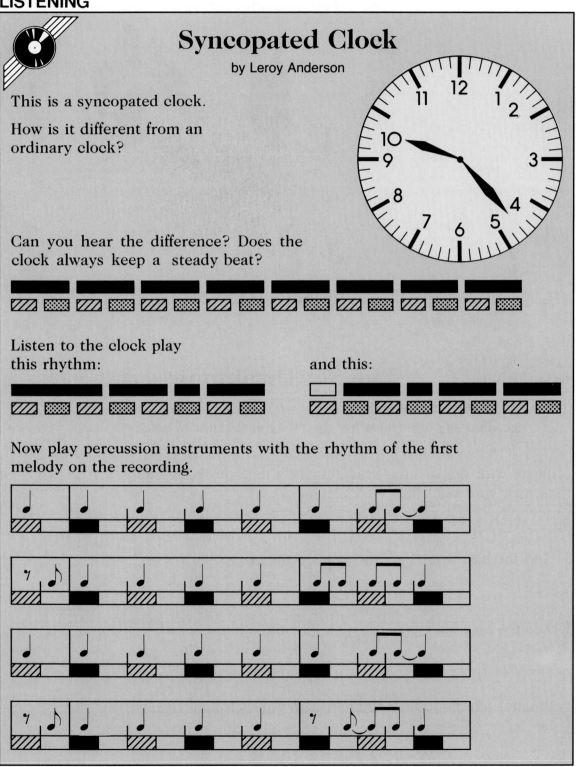

# Syncopated Clock
### by Leroy Anderson

This is a syncopated clock.

How is it different from an ordinary clock?

Can you hear the difference? Does the clock always keep a steady beat?

Listen to the clock play this rhythm:                    and this:

Now play percussion instruments with the rhythm of the first melody on the recording.

# The Second Quarter

## The Set Drummer

Here is a group of rhythms for you to perform. A set drummer might use patterns like these for the rhythm section of a jazz combo.

1. Begin with the "cymbal stick." Lightly tap your right hand against your right leg.

①②③④⑤⑥⑦⑧①②③④⑤⑥⑦⑧

2. Add the bass drum part with your right foot.

① 2 3 4 ⑤ 6 7 8 ① 2 3 4 ⑤ 6 7 8

3. Add the high-hat cymbal rhythm playing "off beats" with left foot.

1 2 ③ 4 5 6 ⑦ 8 1 2 ③ 4 5 6 ⑦ 8

4. Finally, add the snare drum part with your left hand against left leg.

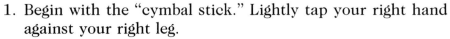

1 2 ③ 4 5 6 ⑦⑧ 1 2 ③ 4 5 6 ⑦⑧

40

Here is a score of the patterns you are playing.

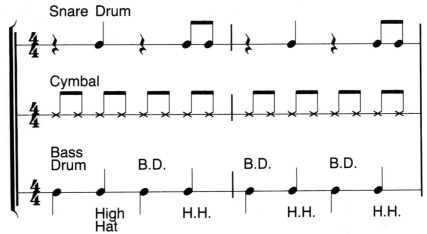

**LISTENING**

# Peter Gunn
by Henry Mancini

This music begins with a series of short sounds:

①②③④⑤⑥⑦⑧①②③④⑤⑥⑦⑧

accompanied by the snare drum in this rhythm.

1   2   ③   4   5   6   ⑦   8   1   2   ③   4   5   6   ⑦   8

Other instruments from the rhythm section pick up the repeated rhythm. They add a repeated melody, or *ostinato*.

Listen for the bass entrance that occurs at the same time:

Listen for the entrance of the brass section. Can you show this rhythm?

# Hand-Clapping Choir

Form a hand-clapping choir and perform the composition on the next page.

Sopranos set the tempo by tapping the pattern of short sounds.

Basses enter next. They establish the meter by accenting the first beat of each measure.

Read the other patterns in relation to the short sounds of the soprano line.

**BASS CLAP**
Cup hands and clap.

**TENOR CLAP**
Clap hands in the usual relaxed way.

**ALTO CLAP**
Use three fingers to strike the opposite open palm.

**SOPRANO CLAP**
Two fingers strike the opposite, very taut palm.

Now add the recorded sounds of the drum set. The drum set will add additional textures as well as more intricate rhythm patterns to your ensemble. Listen to the pattern several times. Then begin.

Work in small groups. Create an original score for hand-clapping choir.

# When Johnny Comes Marching Home

Words and Music by Louis Lambert

As you listen to this song, you can tap the short sounds:

or the beats:

What is the relationship of the short sound to the beat?
The **meter signature** of this song would probably be clearer if it
were written this way: **2**. Why do you suppose it isn't?

## LISTENING

# American Salute

## by Morton Gould

The form of this composition is **theme and variations.** The theme is "When Johnny Comes Marching Home." It is stated seven times.

At the beginning of most statements, a repeated accompaniment figure introduces the theme.

At the end of most statements, the theme is "stretched out" in some way, by adding ornaments or ideas from the melody.

---

Introduction — Full Band

---

Statement 1 — Three Bassoons

---

2. English Horn

3. Bass Winds and Brasses

---

4. Piccolo, Flutes, and Clarinets

---

5. Full Band

---

6. Cornets and Trombone

---

7. Reed Instruments and Xylophone

Coda

# Analyzing Rhythm

Musical rhythm is made up of different parts:

- the underlying steady beat

- the accents, which organize beats into groups

- the underlying shortest sound

- the rhythm of the melody, which is made up of longer and shorter sounds

Can you identify the different parts of rhythm in each of these examples?

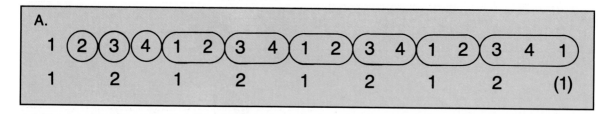

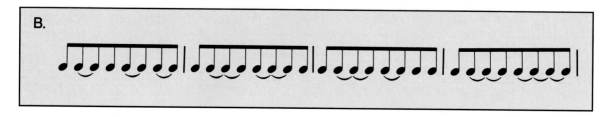

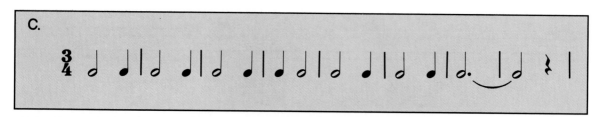

Look at "Are You From Dixie?" Can you read the rhythm as it is shown? If you have problems, rewrite the rhythm of the melody by circling numbers or by tying short sounds together.

# Are You From Dixie?

Words and Music by George L. Cobb

Are you from Dix - ie? I said from Dix - ie!

Where the fields of cot - ton beck-on to me, 

I'm glad to see you. Tell me, how be you 

And the friends I'm long - in' to see? 

If you're from Al - a - ba - ma, Ten - nes - see, or Car - o - line,

An - y place be - low the Ma - son Dix - on line, 

Then you're from Dix - ie. Hur - ray for Dix - ie! 

'Cause I'm from Dix - ie, too.

# Mary and Martha

Spiritual

When studying a melody you need to identify

- the **tonal center**, or **home tone**
- the scale from which the pitches of the melody are drawn
- patterns which move up or down by steps of the scale
- patterns which move up or down by chordal skips

Ma - ry and Mar - tha's just gone a - long,

Ma - ry and Mar - tha's just gone a - long,

Ma - ry and Mar - tha's just gone a - long

To ring those charm - ing bells. Cry - ing

free grace, un - dy - ing love; free grace un - dy - ing love;

Free grace, un - dy - ing love; to ring those charm-ing bells. Oh,

48

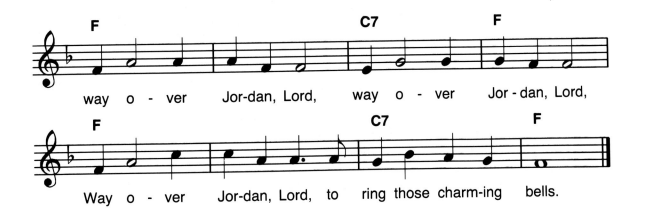

way o - ver Jor-dan, Lord, way o - ver Jor - dan, Lord,

Way o - ver Jor-dan, Lord, to ring those charm-ing bells.

Sing in harmony.

melody

middle part

lower part

49

# Limbo Like Me

Words and Music Adapted by
Massie Patterson and Sammy Heyward

Perform limbo dance steps. Lean back while hopping forward on each beat. Dance under the limbo stick without losing balance.

**Moderato**

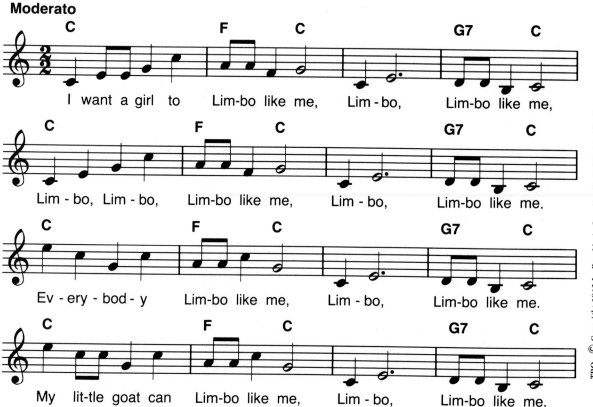

I want a girl to Lim-bo like me, Lim - bo, Lim-bo like me,

Lim - bo, Lim - bo, Lim-bo like me, Lim - bo, Lim-bo like me.

Ev - ery - bod - y Lim-bo like me, Lim - bo, Lim-bo like me.

My lit-tle goat can Lim-bo like me, Lim - bo, Lim-bo like me.

Mon-key try to Lim-bo like me, Lim - bo, Lim-bo like me.

Mon-key no can Lim-bo like me, Lim - bo, Lim-bo like me.

One an' all come Lim-bo like me, Lim - bo, Lim-bo like me.

Lim - bo, Lim-bo like me, Lim - bo, Lim-bo like me.

Use these bells to play an accompaniment:

Phrases 1–7

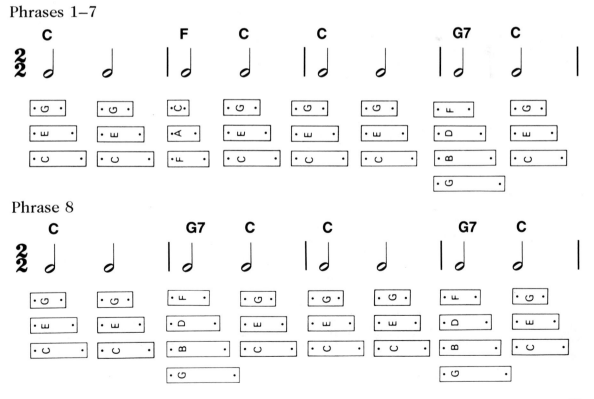

Phrase 8

# Joe Turner

Blues Song

I(**C**)                                  I7(**C7**)

1. They tell me _ Joe Tur-ner's _ come and gone. ____
2. He came here _ with for-ty __ links of chain. ____
3. Joe Tur-ner _ he took my _ man a-way. ____

IV(**F**)                                  I(**C**)

They tell me _ Joe Tur-ner's _ come and gone. ____  
He came here _ with for-ty __ links of chain. ____  ⎫
Joe Tur-ner _ he took my _ man a-way. ____  ⎭

V7(**G7**)                                  I(**C**)

He left me _ here to sing ____ this ____ song.

52

**Improvise** an accompaniment using these bells:

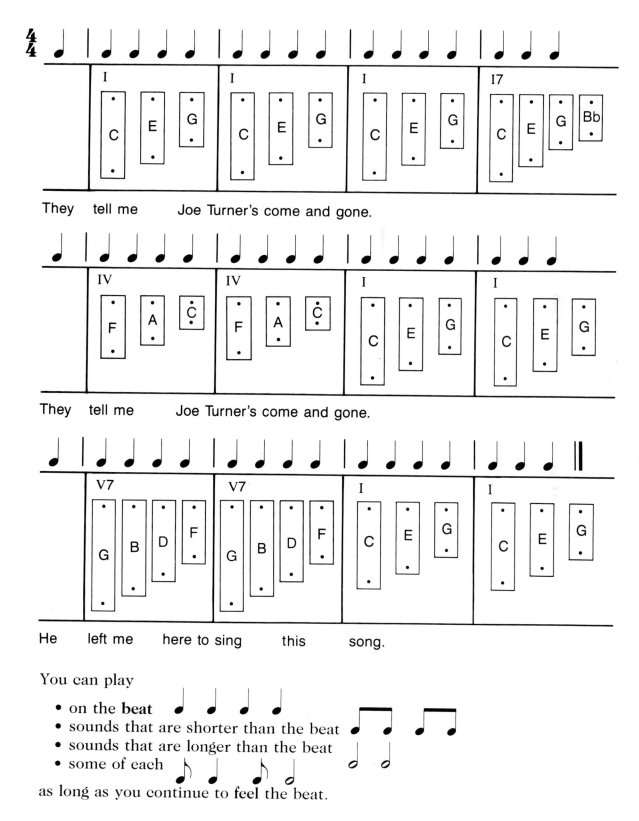

They tell me Joe Turner's come and gone.

They tell me Joe Turner's come and gone.

He left me here to sing this song.

You can play
- on the **beat**
- sounds that are shorter than the beat
- sounds that are longer than the beat
- some of each

as long as you continue to feel the beat.

# The City Blues

U.S. Folk Blues
Words Compiled
by Jerry Silverman
Additional Verses by
Eugene W. Troth

1. Cloud - y   in   the west,        looks   like     rain; ___
2. Went   to   De  -  troit;         it   was     fine, ___

I   spent   all   my   mon - ey   on   the   sub - way   train ___
I   watched the cars   mov - in' off   th' as - sem - bly   line ___

In   New York Cit-y, _____      in   New York Cit-y, _____
In   De - troit Cit-y, _____      in   De - troit Cit-y, _____

In   New   York   Cit - y,   you   real - ly got   to know your   way. _
In   De - troit   Cit - y,   you   real - ly got   to know your   way. _

1.–7.          8.

                              2.   I
                              3.   I     ___

3.   I looped the loop, I rocked and reeled,
     I thought the Cubs played ball in the Marshall Field.
     In the Windy City, in the Windy City,
     In the Windy City, you really got to know your way.

54

4. Went a little south, St. Louis (Loo-ee),
   A piece of Missouri on the Mississippi.
   In old St. Louis, in old St. Louis,
   In old St. Louis, you really got to know your way.

5. I moved on down, New Orleans (Or-leens).
   I had my first taste of its pecan pralines,
   In New Orleans, in New Orleans,
   In New Orleans, you really got to know your way.

6. I headed West, to "L.A."
   It really is a city where it's fun to stay,
   In old "L.A.," in old "L.A."
   In old "L.A.," you really got to know your way.

7. Headed up the coast, "Golden Gate."
   I went out to the wharf to eat a "Fisherman's Plate,"
   In San Francisco, in San Francisco,
   In San Francisco, you really got to know your way.

8. Went on north, Seattle.
   I gave its Space Needle a mighty pull.
   In old Seattle, in old Seattle,
   In old Seattle, you really got to know your way.

Compare these two scales.

Improvise a melody. Use the pitches of the blues scale.

Use any of these rhythm patterns,
or make up your own.

Someone may play
the autoharp.

# Jesu, Joy of Man's Desiring

from *Cantata No. 147*

by Johann Sebastian Bach

"Imitation is a form of flattery."

What do you think is meant by this phrase? One way musicians have flattered each other is by imitating or copying the music of other composers. One of the most copied composers is Johann Sebastian Bach. Although he lived in the eighteenth century, composers and arrangers have been listening to his music and imitating his style for over two hundred years.

Listen to "Jesu, Joy of Man's Desiring," as originally composed by Bach. As you hear the recording, pay particular attention to

• the bass accompaniment, which begins like this:

• Melody A, which begins like this:

• Melody B, which begins like this:

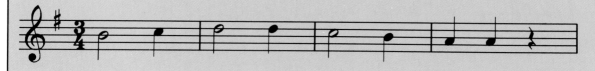

Follow the "mini-score" as you listen. All of Melody B is written out. What is happening during the measures of rest? What happens to the bass accompaniment line?

Many composers have borrowed ideas from Bach. Listen to four versions of this composition, each arranged by a different person. What changes do you notice in the form? the melody? rhythm? instrumentation? accompaniment?

A composer must make decisions when composing music for an orchestra. One important decision is the choice of instruments to perform each part: the melody, the countermelodies or ornamental parts, and the accompaniment.

Listen to the way one composer, Benjamin Britten, decided to use instrument groups in "The Young Person's Guide to the Orchestra." Compare the instrument sounds that you hear.

# The Young Person's Guide to the Orchestra

## (Variations and Fugue on a Theme of Purcell)

### by Benjamin Britten

Listen to "The Young Person's Guide to the Orchestra." The first section is based on a theme by Henry Purcell, an English composer who lived three hundred years ago. The theme is played first by full orchestra, then by different instrument groups.

Now follow Britten's variations on the theme, each played on a particular instrument. Excerpts from several variations are shown below. As you listen, imagine what each might sound like if it were played on another instrument.

The **woodwind** section begins with flutes:

*Next are the* **strings**, starting with violins:

The **brass** sequence includes a variation played on trumpets:

Final variations are on **percussion.** Timpani begins:

After the variations, another theme is played as a **fugue.** The composition ends with a return to Purcell's theme.

# The Orchestra

The orchestra has grown from a small group of instrumentalists to a group of more than one hundred musicians. Compare the sizes of the orchestras of these composers.

Vivaldi (c.1675–1741)  ●

Rossini (1792–1868)  ○

Grofé (1892–1972)  X

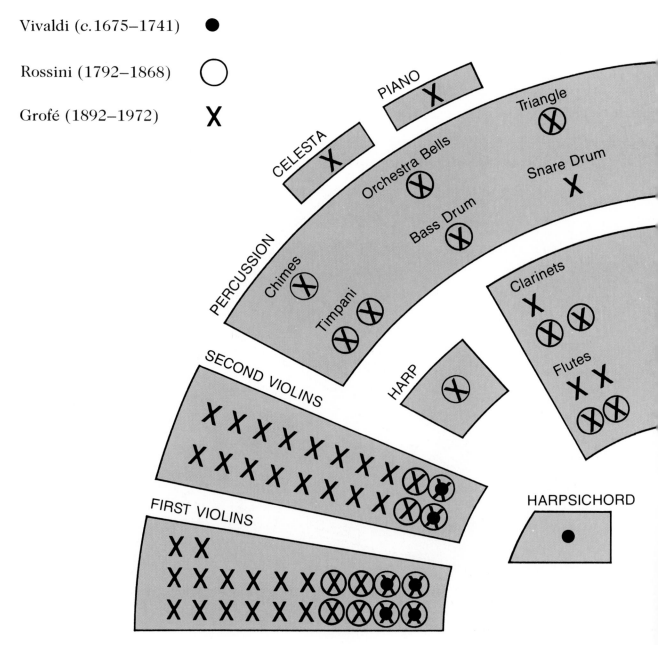

Three composers who lived in three different centuries all wrote music describing a storm. Listen to the three compositions. What differences and similarities do you notice?

"Summer"
from *The Four Seasons*
by Antonio Vivaldi

"The Storm"
from *William Tell Overture*
by Gioacchino Rossini

"Cloudburst"
from *Grand Canyon Suite*
by Ferde Grofé

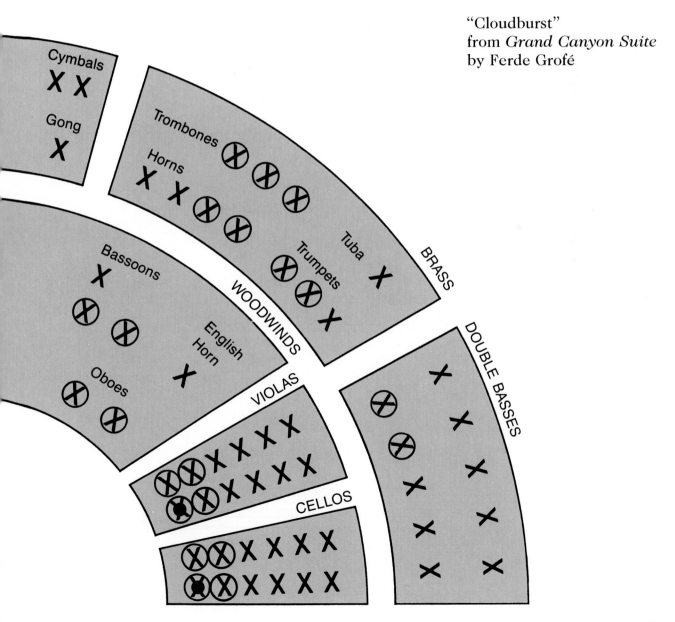

# Amazing Grace

Early American Melody

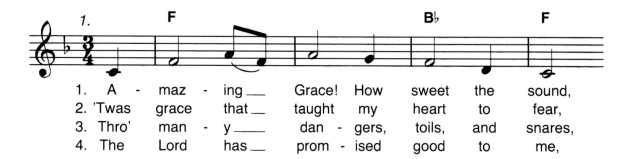

1. A - maz - ing __ Grace! How sweet the sound,
2. 'Twas grace that __ taught my heart to fear,
3. Thro' man - y __ dan - gers, toils, and snares,
4. The Lord has __ prom - ised good to me,

That saved a __ wretch like me! __
And grace my __ fears re - lieved; __
I have al - read - y come; __
His word my __ hope se - cures; __

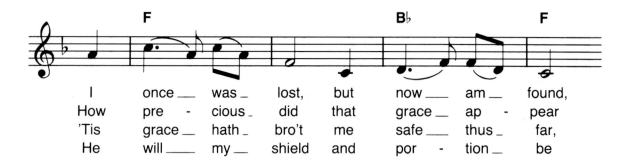

I once __ was __ lost, but now __ am __ found,
How pre - cious __ did that grace __ ap - pear
'Tis grace __ hath __ bro't me safe __ thus __ far,
He will __ my __ shield and por - tion __ be

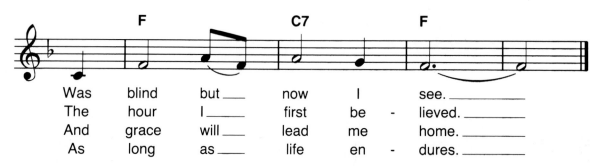

Was blind but __ now I see. __
The hour I __ first be - lieved. __
And grace will __ lead me home. __
As long as __ life en - dures. __

64

# Musical Decisions

What makes each version different?

Version 1

Version 2

Version 3

Version 4

Version 5

Is the music sung or played as written? Is it improvised?
Do you like the music best when it's

- faster?
- louder?
- *legato?*

- slower?
- softer?
- *staccato?*

Why?

Which instruments do you like best? Why?

# Dona Nobis Pacem

Three-part Canon

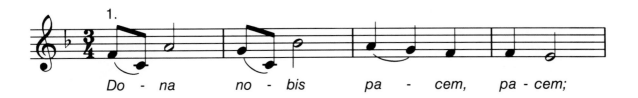

Do - na no - bis pa - cem, pa - cem;

Do - na __ no - bis pa - cem.

Do - na no - bis pa - cem;

Do - na no - bis pa - cem.

Do - na no - bis __ pa - cem;

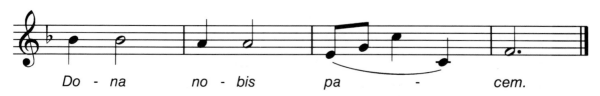

Do - na no - bis pa - cem.

# Musical Choices

Follow each colored line as you sing in unison: red, blue, green. Sing it in three parts. Each group follows one of the colors. Notice how the parts fit together.

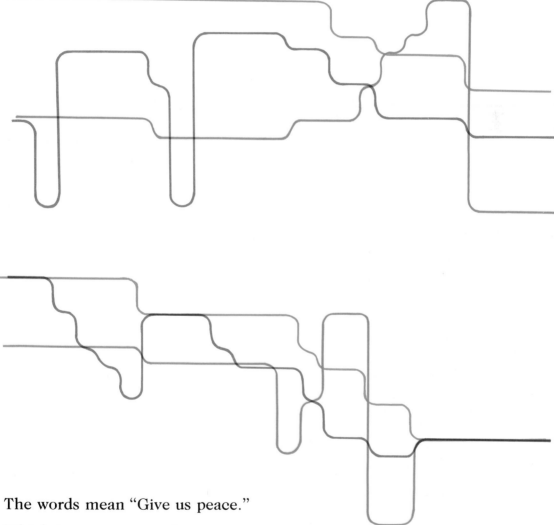

The words mean "Give us peace."

Which is more appropriate:

- a fast **tempo** or a slow tempo?
- a light accompaniment or a heavy accompaniment?
- a *legato* style or a *staccato* style?

Listen to several different versions. Which are appropriate ways of performing the song? Why?

Two-beat Pattern

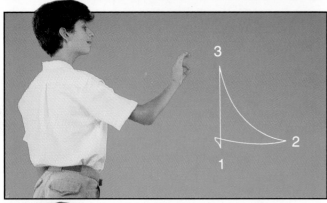

Three-beat Pattern

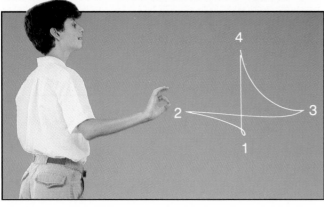

Four-beat Pattern

Which pattern fits
- Seventy-Six Trombones
- Goodnight, My Someone
- All Through the Night

# All Through the Night

Welsh Melody

Conduct this song.    Which pattern will you use?

1. Sleep, my child and peace at-tend thee ⎱
2. While the moon her   watch is keep-ing ⎰   All  through  the   night;

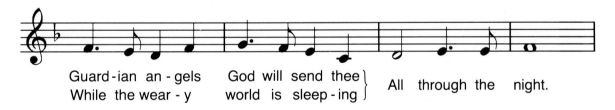

Guard-ian an - gels     God will send thee ⎱
While the wear - y      world is sleep-ing ⎰   All  through  the   night.

Soft the drow-sy  hours are creep-ing,  Hill and vale in   slum-ber sleep-ing,
O'er thy spir - it     gent - ly steal-ing,   Vi-sions of de - light re-veal-ing,

I   my lov-ing     vig - il keep-ing ⎱
Breathes a sure and   ho - ly feel-ing ⎰   All  through  the   night.

69

# Review 2

## Nutcracker Suite
### (excerpts)
by Peter Ilyich Tchaikovsky

Peter Tchaikovsky composed this ballet in 1891.

How does Tchaikovsky achieve excitement in "Trepak," or "Russian Dance"?

Look at this theme. Check the dynamics and articulation.

Listen to three flutes play "Dance of the Mirlitons," or "Dance of the Reed Pipes."

What instrument plays this theme?

What instrument family is featured in "Arabian Dance"?

Tchaikovsky was the first composer to use the celesta. He used it in "Dance of the Sugarplum Fairy."

# The Third Quarter

## Come, Follow Me

Round by John Hilton

Can you tap the
shortest sound
with one hand
and
tap the rhythm
of the words
with the other?

Start with the
shortest sound.

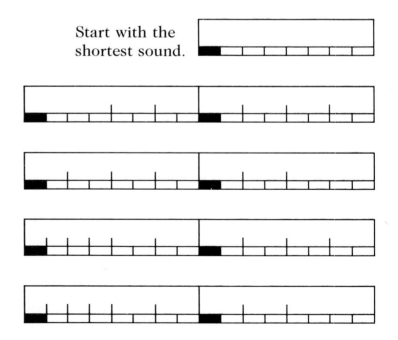

1.

Come, fol - low, fol - low, fol - low,

Fol - low, fol - low, fol - low me!

2.

Whith - er shall I fol - low, fol - low, fol - low,

Whith - er shall I fol - low, fol - low thee?

3.

To the green - wood, to the green - wood,

To the green - wood, green - wood tree.

This song can be sung as a three-part round. Follow the lines below. Can your ears hear what your eyes see?

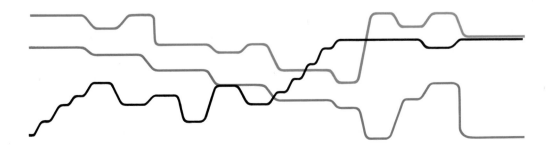

# Oh, Mary, Don't You Weep

Spiritual

One of these chants is **syncopated.**
Can you tell which one by studying the Rhythm Rulers?

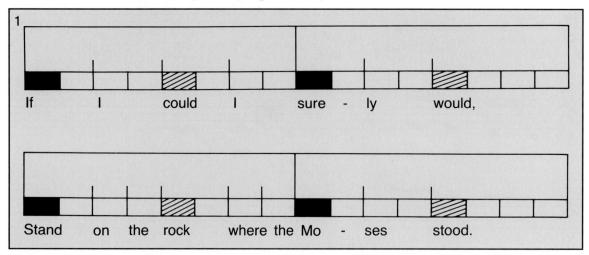

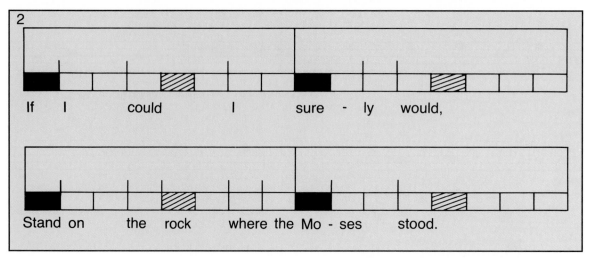

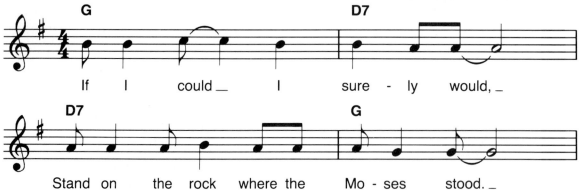

74

Pha-roah's ar - my got drown-ded, Oh, Ma-ry, don't you weep.

Oh, Ma - ry, don't you weep, don't you mourn,

Oh, Ma - ry, don't you weep, don't you mourn.

Pha-roah's ar - my got drown-ded, Oh, Ma-ry, don't you weep.

## LISTENING

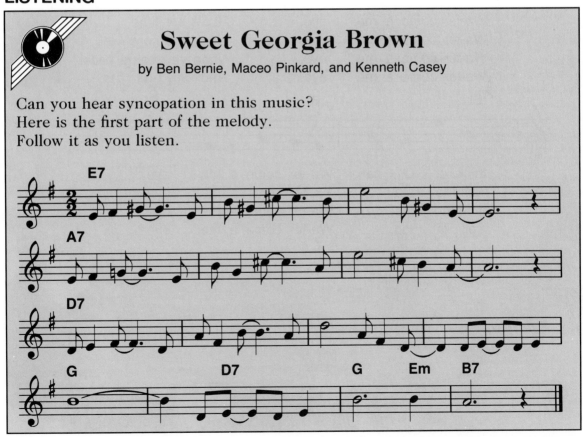

# Sweet Georgia Brown

by Ben Bernie, Maceo Pinkard, and Kenneth Casey

Can you hear syncopation in this music?
Here is the first part of the melody.
Follow it as you listen.

# Water Come a Me Eye

Words Adapted                                              Jamaican Folk Song

Listen to the recording. Tap the **short sounds**, played on the maracas. Then chant the rhythm of the words as you continue to tap.

1. Ev - ery time    I    think    of    Li - za
2. Don't  know why  you   went   a - way, __
3. Time   go slow when   love   is   past, __
4. Lis - ten 'cause I'm  call - in'   you, __

Wa-ter come a me    eye.        Ev - ery time    I
Wa-ter come a me    eye.        When you com - in'
Wa-ter come a me    eye.        When you come back,
Wa-ter come a me    eye.        And   my heart  is

think  of   Li - za   Wa-ter come a me    eye.
home to    stay? _    Wa-ter come a me    eye.
time go    fast, __   Wa-ter come a me    eye.
call - in'  too, __   Wa-ter come a me    eye.

*Refrain*

Come back, Li-za, come back girl, Wa-ter come a me eye.

Come back, Li-za, come back girl, Wa-ter come a me eye.

## LISTENING

# Brazilian Dance

### from *Three Dances for Orchestra*

by Camargo Guarnieri

Much of the excitement of this lively **samba** comes from its driving rhythms based on short sounds. Listen to the whole dance. As you listen, try lightly tapping the shortest sounds.

① ② ③ ④ ⑤ ⑥ ⑦ ⑧ ① ② ③ ④ ⑤ ⑥ ⑦ ⑧

Can you continue to sense the shortest sounds even when they are not heard in the music?

This entire composition is based on two thematic ideas.

Theme 1      1 2 3 4 5 ⑥⑦⑧①②③④⑤⑥⑦⑧

Accompaniment ①②③④⑤⑥⑦⑧①②③④⑤⑥⑦⑧

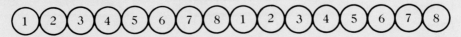

Listen to the dance again. As you listen to the opening section, try tapping either the rhythm of the theme or the rhythm of the accompaniment.

Can you hear the introduction of the second theme? It is played first by trombones. This time the driving pattern of short sounds is in the accompaniment.

Theme 2      1 2 3 4 5 6 ⑦⑧①②③④⑤⑥⑦⑧

Accompaniment ①②③④⑤⑥⑦⑧①②③④⑤⑥⑦⑧

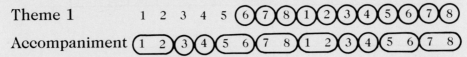

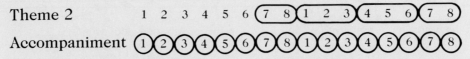

Near the middle of the composition, the strings play the most complete statement of Theme 2. Is the accompaniment the same as before?

# Go Down the Wishin' Road

Calypso Folk Song
Words and Music Arranged by Albert Stanton,
Jessie Cavanaugh,
and Blake Alphonso Higgs

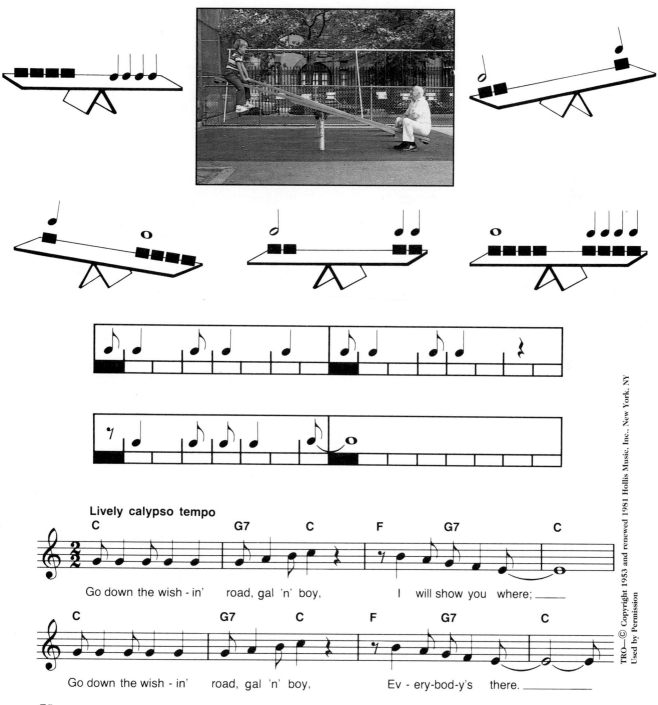

Lively calypso tempo

Go down the wish - in' road, gal 'n' boy,    I will show you where; _____

Go down the wish - in' road, gal 'n' boy,    Ev - ery-bod-y's    there. _____

You're gon - na find 'em one by one, boy! ___

Find 'em two by two, gal 'n' boy,

Find 'em three by three, boy! ___ Find 'em four by four.

Gal 'n' boy, go out ___ in the moon - light _____

Un - der - neath a trop - i - cal sky. _____

You're gon - na catch 'em one by one, boy! ___

Catch 'em two by two, gal 'n' boy,

Catch 'em three by three, boy! _____

Catch 'em four by four.

# Shenandoah

American Sea Chantey

Some of the measures on these musical seesaws are in $\frac{3}{4}$, some in $\frac{4}{4}$.

Can you identify the meter signature for each group of notes?

Set ♪ as the shortest sound and read the rhythms on all the seesaws. Move from one seesaw to the next without interrupting the flow of the rhythm.

Locate the note groups in the song.

1. Oh, Shen - an - doah, __ I long to hear you,
2. Oh, Shen - an - doah, __ I love your daugh-ter,
3. Oh, Shen - an - doah, __ I'm bound to leave you,

A - way, you roll - in' riv - er,

80

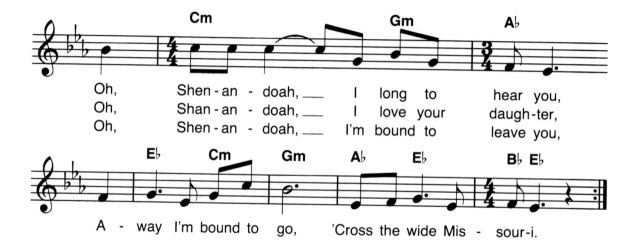

Oh,          Shen - an - doah, ___   I   long   to       hear you,
Oh,          Shan - an - doah, ___   I   love  your       daugh-ter,
Oh,          Shen - an - doah, ___   I'm bound  to       leave you,

A - way I'm bound to   go,      'Cross the wide Mis - sour-i.

Listen to "Shenandoah." Is it based on a major or a minor scale? Check your answer by using the Scale Finders and the Chromatic Scale Ruler.

- Locate the tonal center of the melody. It is usually the last pitch.
- Circle its name on your Chromatic Scale Ruler.
- Locate all *different* pitches used in the melody. Circle the names of these pitches on the Chromatic Scale Ruler, starting with the tonal center as the lowest pitch.
- Place one of the Scale Finders over the Chromatic Scale Ruler so that the tonal center appears in the first cutout of the finder.
- If you chose the proper scale, every pitch you circled should show in the cutouts of the Scale Finder.

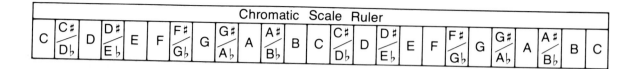

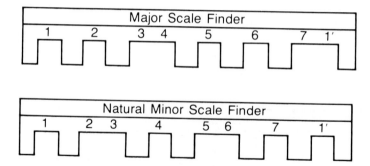

If this is a

| | C | C#/Db | D | D#/Eb | E | F | F#/Gb | G | G#/Ab | A | A#/Bb | B | C |
|---|---|---|---|---|---|---|---|---|---|---|---|---|---|
| CHROMATIC SCALE | C | C#/Db | D | D#/Eb | E | F | F#/Gb | G | G#/Ab | A | A#/Bb | B | C |
| MAJOR SCALE | C | | D | | E | F | | G | | A | | B | C |
| MINOR SCALE | C | | D | Eb | | F | | G | Ab | | Bb | | C |
| PENTATONIC SCALE | C | | D | | E | | | G | | A | | | C |
| WHOLE-TONE SCALE | C | | D | | E | | F# | | G# | | A# | | C |

Then can you

. . . describe two ways that all scales are the *same*?

. . . describe two ways in which each is *different*?

. . . make a definition of a scale?

Play the song on the next page using each of these scales. Discuss the effect a scale has on the mood of the melody.

Make up your own six-pitch scale. Play the song using this new scale. What effect does it have on the mood?

# When I First Came to This Land

American Ballad

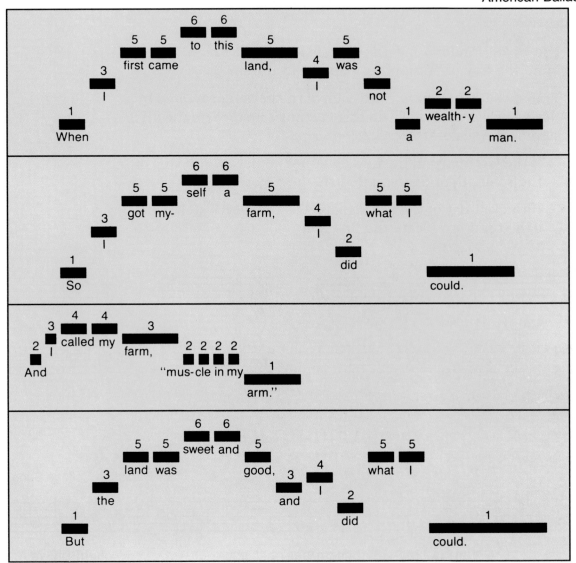

Additional Verses:

2. So I built myself a shack . . . and I called my shack, "break
   my back."

3. So I got myself a cow . . . and I called my cow, "no milk
   now."

4. So I got myself a horse . . . and I called my horse, "horse,
   of course."

5. So I got myself a wife . . . and I called my wife, "love of my
   life."

6. So I got myself a son . . . and I called my son, "my work's
   done."

# Scales and Keys

1. Use Scale Finders and the Chromatic Scale Ruler. Determine the **key** of "Chumbara" and "Old Abram Brown."

2. **Transpose** "Chumbara" into each of the keys represented by these key signatures. To do this you must first locate the first step of the scale—the tonal center.

   - ♯ If the last **sharp** in the key signature is the seventh step of the scale, then can you find the first step?

   - ♭ If the last **flat** in the key signature is the fourth step, what can you do to locate the first step?

## Chumbara

Canadian College Song

Chum-ba - ra, _____ chum-ba - ra,    chum-ba - ra, _____ chum-ba - ra,

Chum-ba-ra,__ chum-ba-ra, chum-chum-chum-chum-chum-chum-chum-chum,

Chum-ba - ra, _____ chum-ba - ra,    chum-ba - ra, _____ chum-ba - ra,

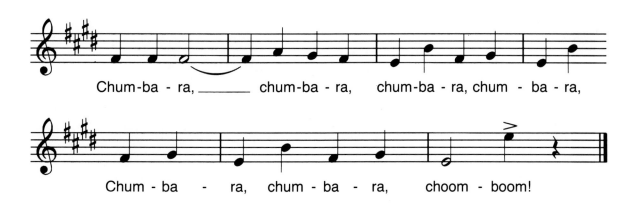

Chum-ba - ra, _____ chum-ba - ra, chum-ba - ra, chum - ba - ra,

Chum - ba - ra, chum - ba - ra, choom - boom!

# Old Abram Brown

Words Anonymous

Music by Benjamin Britten

Transpose "Old Abram Brown" into the *minor* keys represented by the key signatures on page 84. First locate the tonal center.

- ♯ If the last sharp in the **key signature** is the second step of the minor scale, locate the first step.

- ♭ If the last flat in the key signature is the sixth step of the minor scale, locate the first step.

Old     A-bram Brown is dead and gone, you'll nev - er see him more.

He     used to wear a long brown coat that but-toned down be-fore.

Choose one of the songs and one of the scales; play the song in that scale using bells or other pitched instruments.

# Arirang

Words Adapted

Korean Folk Song

Before you begin to learn this song, determine the scale on which it is based. Use the Chromatic Scale Ruler and the Scale Finders to help you make the decision.

1. A - ri - rang,— A - ri - rang,— A - ri - rang,— A - ri - rang,—
2. A - ri - rang,— A - ri - rang,— A - ri - rang,— A - ri - rang,—

A - ri - rang,— A - ri - rang,— A - ri - rang fair.
A - ri - rang,— A - ri - rang,— A - ri - rang fair.

Through the pass — I watch you — go — there. _____
Here I wait for you, wait, wait — and — stare. _____

A - ri - rang,— A - ri - rang,— A - ri - rang fair.
A - ri - rang,— A - ri - rang,— A - ri - rang fair.

# The Cage

Words and Music by Charles Ives

A leopard went around his cage
from one side to the other side; he stopped
only when the keeper came around with meat.
A boy who had been there three hours began to wonder,
"Is life anything like that?"

What kind of a melody would you compose for this poem?
Would you use any special musical elements to help express the
feelings and ideas of the story?

Listen to the setting of this poem by the composer Charles Ives.
He used these scales as the basis for his song.

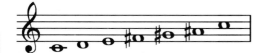 

Did Ives organize any musical elements in the same way you
suggested?

# Frère Jacques

French Folk Tune

*Frère Jacques, Frère Jacques,*
*Dormez-vous? Dormez-vous?*
*Sonnez les matines, sonnez les matines:*
*Ding, ding, dong. Ding, ding, dong.*

Study each version of this familiar tune. On what scale is each based?

88

Version 4

## LISTENING

# Frère Jean Jacques

by Jean Jacques Perrey

When composers create compositions, some of the decisions that must be made relate to the kinds of melodies they wish to compose.

- What kind of scale will be the basis for the melody?
- In what key will it be written? Will it remain in the same key throughout the composition?
- Will the melody be original—newly written—or should it be borrowed?
- Once the initial melody has been presented, should it be repeated exactly, with variations, or should a different melody be introduced?

Listen to a composition for **synthesizer** written by a contemporary American composer. How did he answer these questions as he developed his composition?

Create your own arrangement of *"Frère Jacques."* The accompaniment is provided for you. The form is **A B A C A D A.** Listen carefully to the recorded accompaniment. Can you tell which scale you should use for each section?

# This Old Hammer

American Work Song

**Harmony** results whenever two strands of sound occur at the same time. Learn to sing "This Old Hammer." Then make your own arrangement by combining several strands of sound in different ways. Follow the suggestions on the next page.

**Gm**
This old ham-mer _____ killed John Hen-ry, _____

**D7** **Gm**
This old ham-mer _____ killed John Hen-ry, _____

**Gm**
This old ham-mer _____ killed John Hen-ry, _____

**Gm** **D7** **Gm**
But it won't kill me, _____ won't kill me. _____

Sing a song in **canon.**

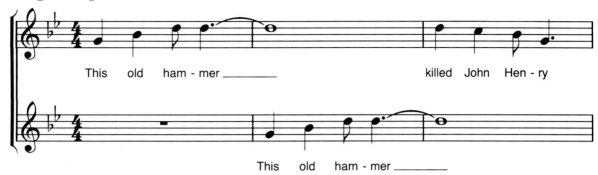

This old ham - mer _____ killed John Hen - ry

This old ham - mer _____

Some people with low voices might add a **drone.**

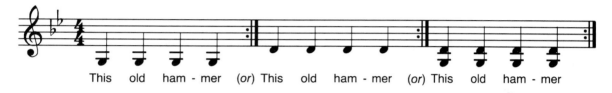

This old ham - mer (*or*) This old ham - mer (*or*) This old ham - mer

Or try an **ostinato,** repeating a pattern like this one over and over.

killed John Hen - ry John.

Or create **polyphony.** Add another melody that "fits."

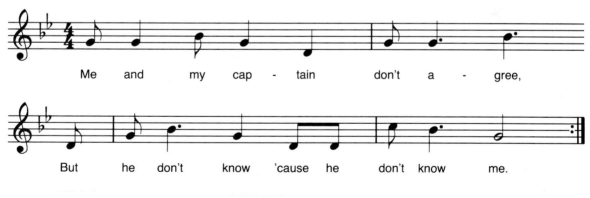

Me and my cap - tain don't a - gree,

But he don't know 'cause he don't know me.

91

# The Swan

Traditional Round

You've been singing rounds for a long time. Singing in round is one way to produce harmony.

Sing this song as a two-part round.

Sweet-ly the swan sings  Do - de - ah - do,  do - de - ah - do,  do - de - ah - do.

When the voices are combined, this harmony results. The voices are sounding in thirds.

Many rounds produce thirds. Review the following.

> "Frère Jacques"
> "Three Blind Mice"
> "Lovely Evening"

Can you tell when the thirds occur?

Sing "The Swan" again, this time as a three-part round. Now the voices are sounding in **triads**, or chords with three pitches. How many thirds are in each triad?

The names of the chords are written in Roman numerals. Why do you suppose they are named IV, III, II, and I?

92

# Hush Little Baby

Traditional

Now that you have the "sound of thirds" in your ears, try harmonizing this old folk tune in thirds. Start by reviewing the melody.

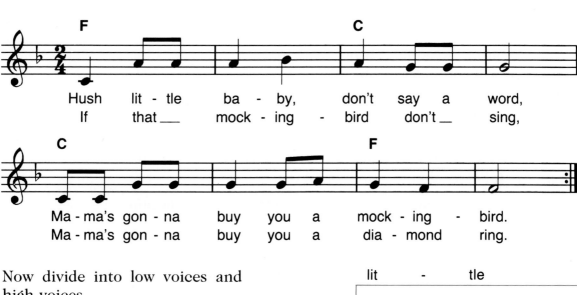

Hush lit - tle ba - by, don't say a word,
If that __ mock - ing - bird don't __ sing,

Ma - ma's gon - na buy you a mock - ing - bird.
Ma - ma's gon - na buy you a dia - mond ring.

Now divide into low voices and high voices.

Everyone begin in **unison** on C.
Low voices continue to sing the melody.

High voices "hop up" to high C on the word "little" and continue to sing the melody from that pitch.

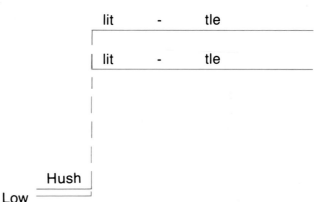

Try something else.
Begin in unison again.
This time, high voices sing the original melody.
Low voices stay on middle C.
Continue to sing the melody, moving up and down from that pitch.

You've sung "upside-down thirds"!
What else might this **interval** be called?

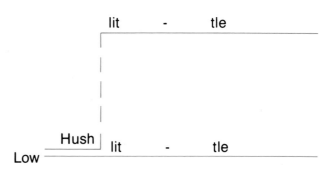

93

# Harmonizing With Parallel Motion

Try harmonizing songs you know "by ear."

- Sing "When I First Came to This Land."
  Begin in thirds. End each phrase in unison.
  When will you need to sing a sixth?
- Sing "Oh, Mary Don't You Weep."
  Begin in sixths.
  When do you need to change to thirds?

You've discovered the pleasing sounds that result when you sing in **parallel motion** in thirds or sixths.

Now try singing "French Cathedrals," moving in parallel motion at the interval of a fourth.

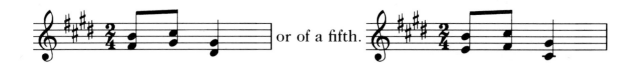

or of a fifth.

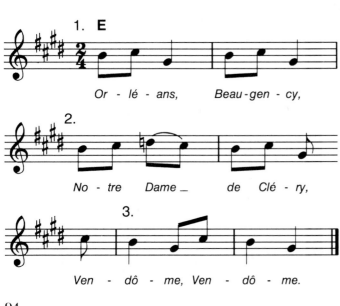

1. E

Or - lé - ans, Beau - gen - cy,

2.

No - tre Dame __ de Clé - ry,

3.

Ven - dô - me, Ven - dô - me.

94

# Glockenjodler

Austrian Folk Song
Arranged by Egon Kraus

# The Alphabet

Music Attributed to Wolfgang Amadeus Mozart

# Exsultate, Jubilate

## Third Movement

by W. A. Mozart

# Sun Magic

Words and Music by Donovan Leitch

4. The sea is a very, very old man,
   Deeper than the deepest blue.
   The sea is a very, very old man,
   Deeper than the deepest blue,
   Deeper than the deepest blue.

5. The moon is a typical lady,
   I watch her wax and wane.
   The moon is a typical lady,
   I watch her wax and wane,
   I watch her wax and wane.

6. A star is so very far away, love,
   Just between you and me.
   A star is so very far away, love,
   Just between you and me,
   Just between you and me.

# Review 3

## Down the River

Traditional

G        C    G

The riv-er is up, and the chan-nel is deep, The

G        D7        G

wind is stead-y and strong; _

1. Oh, won't we have a
2. Oh, Di - nah, put the
3. The waves do splash from

C    G    D7       G

jol - ly good time,
hoe - cake on, } As we go sail-ing a - long. ___
shore _ to shore,

*Refrain*   G         C

Down the riv - er, oh, down the riv - er, Oh,

D7        G

down the riv - er we go - o - o;

G        C

Down the riv - er, oh, down the riv - er, Oh,

D7        G

down the O - hi - o! ___

100

# Vive l'amour

Traditional

**With animation**

G     C     D7     G

Let ev - ery good fel - low now join in a song,

G     D7     G

Vi - ve la com - pa - gnie!

G     C     D7     G

Suc - cess to each oth - er and pass it a - long,

G     D7     G

Vi - ve la com - pa - gnie! _____

*Refrain*

G     C

Vi - ve l'a - vi - ve l'a - vi - ve l'a - mour,

D7     G

Vi - ve l'a - vi - ve l'a - vi - ve l'a - mour,

G     C

Vi - ve l'a - mour, Vi - ve l'a - mour,

D7     G

Vi - ve la com - pa - gnie! _____

# The Fourth Quarter

Which of these are ideas?
What ideas are expressed?

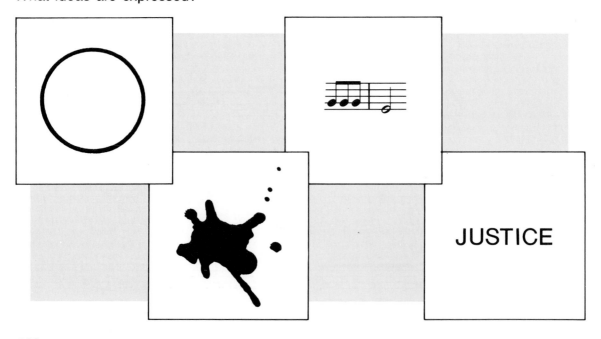

JUSTICE

# The Artist Expresses Ideas

Notice how the artist begins with a single idea and extends it into a complete work of art.

*Electric Prism,* 1914, by Sonia Delaunay (1885–1979)
Private collection, Paris.

# The Dancer Expresses Ideas

Notice that the dancer begins with a single movement idea and extends it into a series of movements.

# The Poet Expresses Ideas

Read the poem. Notice how the poet begins with a single idea and extends it into a complete poem.

## Beauty

by E-Yeh-Shure

Beauty is seen
In the sunlight,
The trees, the birds,
Corn growing and people working
Or dancing for their harvest.

Beauty is heard
In the night,
Wind sighing, rain falling,
Or a singer chanting
Anything in earnest.

Beauty is in yourself.
Good deeds, happy thoughts
That repeat themselves
In your dreams,
In your work,
And even in your rest.

105

# I Walk the Unfrequented Road

Words by Frederick L. Hosmer

American Folk Hymn

**Gm**                          **Dm**

1. I walk the un - fre - quent - ed ___ road
2. A beau - ty spring - time ___ nev - er ___ knew
3. I face the hills, the ___ streams, the ___ woods

**Gm**                          **Gm**

With o - pen eye and ear;
Haunts all the qui - et ways,
And feel with all a - kin;

**Gm**                          **Dm**

I ___ watch a - field the farm - er ___ load
And ___ sweet - er ___ shines the land - scape ___ thro'
My ___ heart ex - pands; their for - ti - tude

**Gm**                    **Dm**   **Gm**

The boun - ty of ___ the year.
Its veil of au - tumn haze.
And peace and joy ___ flow in.

# Jolly Polka

## from *Mala Suite*

### by Witold Lutoslawski

How many different musical ideas did the composer use to create this short "jolly polka"? Listen to decide. You will hear call numbers on the recording. The numbered boxes on the page match the call numbers you hear. Be ready to answer the questions in each of the boxes after you have listened to the complete composition.

1. Clarinets, trombones, and strings introduce an accompaniment figure. This musical idea is then stated:

How many times is it heard?

2. How does this musical idea compare with what you heard in Box 1?

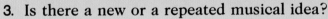

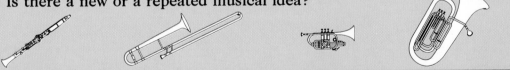

3. Is there a new or a repeated musical idea?

4. What has changed?

5. How is the composition brought to a close?

A song can be built around one musical idea, two musical ideas, or several musical ideas. Each idea can be repeated exactly, repeated with variation, or extended. New ideas can be introduced to provide contrast.

## LISTENING

# Emmanuel Road

Listen to *Emmanuel Road*.
How many ideas are used?
Are the ideas repeated? extended? varied?

Perform this dance with "Take Time in Life."

**Beat 1** With right foot, step forward and right.
**Beat 2** Bring left foot next to right foot.
**Beat 3** Cross left foot over right foot.
**Beat 4** Move right foot to right of left foot.
Repeat, reversing feet (start on left foot).

# Take Time in Life

African Dance Song

Learn the musical idea
on which this song is based:

Identify the ways this idea has been repeated, varied, and
extended to create the complete song.

Use this information to help you learn to sing the song.
Apply the reading skills you have developed.

1. I was pass - ing by, My broth - er called me in,
2. I was pass - ing by, My un - cle called me in,
3. I was pass - ing by, Some peo - ple called me in,

And he said to me, You bet - ter take time in life.
And he said to me, My neph - ew, take time in life,
And they said to me, My young man, take time in life,

Peo - ple take time in life, Peo - ple take time in life,
Neph - ew, take time in life, Neph - ew, take time in life,
Young man, take time in life, Young man, take time in life,

Peo - ple
Neph - ew,  } take time in life, 'Cause you got far 'way to go.
Young man,

# Aye, Aye, Aye-Aye (The Limerick Song)

Traditional

Apply your knowledge of form, rhythm, and melody to learn this song.

*Refrain*

**F**      **A7**      **B♭**

Aye,    aye,    aye - aye, _____

**C7**      **F**

In   Tex-as they   claim they grow   big - ger, _____

**F**      **C7**

So    tell me an - oth-er that's   worse than the   t'oth-er,

**C7**      **F**      *Fine*

And   dust it   all    o - ver with   sug - ar. _____

*Verse*   **F**      **C7**

1. A    tu - tor who   toot-ed the    flute, _____
2. There   was a young   lad - y named   Wright, ____
3. There   was _ a    din - er named   Drew, ____

**C7**      **F**

Tried to    tu - tor two   toot-ers to     toot, _____
Who _   trav-eled much fast - er than   light. _____
Who _   found an   old   shoe in his    stew. _____

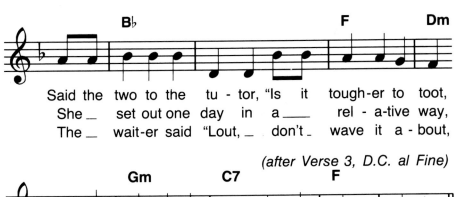

Said the two to the tu - tor, "Is it tough-er to toot,
She _ set out one day in a ___ rel - a-tive way,
The _ wait-er said "Lout, _ don't _ wave it a - bout,

*(after Verse 3, D.C. al Fine)*

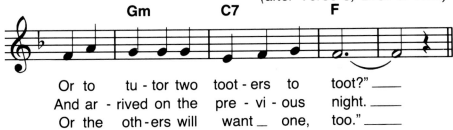

Or to tu - tor two toot - ers to toot?" ___
And ar - rived on the pre - vi - ous night. ___
Or the oth - ers will want _ one, too." ___

# Limericks

A limerick is a special kind of nonsensical rhyme. Each one fol-lows the same rhythmic organization. Edward Lear was one of the best limerick writers. Add these as new verses to "Aye, Aye, Aye-Aye."

There was a Young Lady whose chin
Resembled the point of a pin;
So she had it made sharp,
And purchased a harp,
And played several tunes with her chin.

There was an Old Man in a boat,
Who said, "I'm afloat! I'm afloat!"
When they said, "No, you ain't!"
He was ready to faint,
That unhappy Old Man in a boat.

Write your own limerick.
Be sure it matches the rhyming form
and rhythmic organization.
Try these for starters:

There was a ballplayer named Dan . . .
or
There once was a marvelous car . . .

117

# Minuet

from *Eine Kleine Nachtmusik*

by Wolfgang Amadeus Mozart

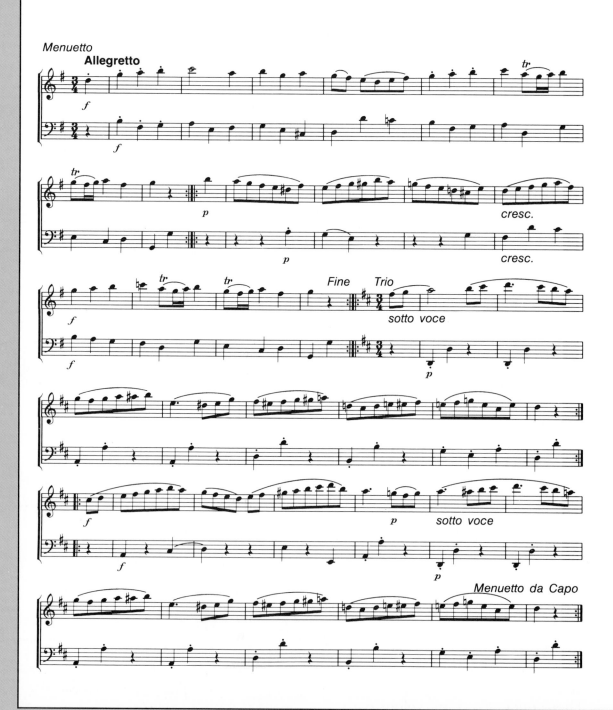

# Take Time in Life

African Dance Song

Learn the musical idea
on which this song is based:

Identify the ways this idea has been repeated, varied, and
extended to create the complete song.

Use this information to help you learn to sing the song.
Apply the reading skills you have developed.

1. I was pass - ing by, My broth - er called me in,
2. I was pass - ing by, My un - cle called me in,
3. I was pass - ing by, Some peo-ple called me in,

And he said to me, You bet - ter take time in life.
And he said to me, My neph - ew, take time in life,
And they said to me, My young man, take time in life,

Peo - ple take time in life, Peo - ple take time in life,
Neph - ew, take time in life, Neph - ew, take time in life,
Young man, take time in life, Young man, take time in life,

Peo - ple
Neph - ew, } take time in life, 'Cause you got far 'way to go.
Young man,

# Symphony No. 5
## First Movement
by Ludwig van Beethoven

Listen to the way one of the most famous musical ideas of our time is developed into a complete composition.

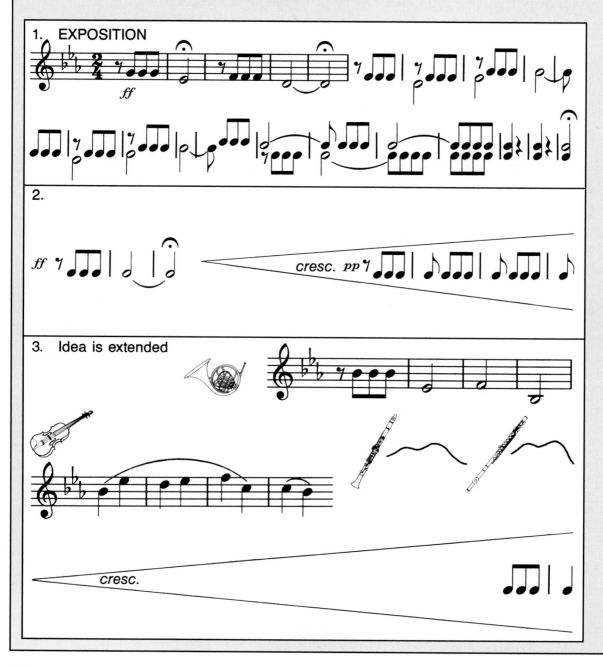

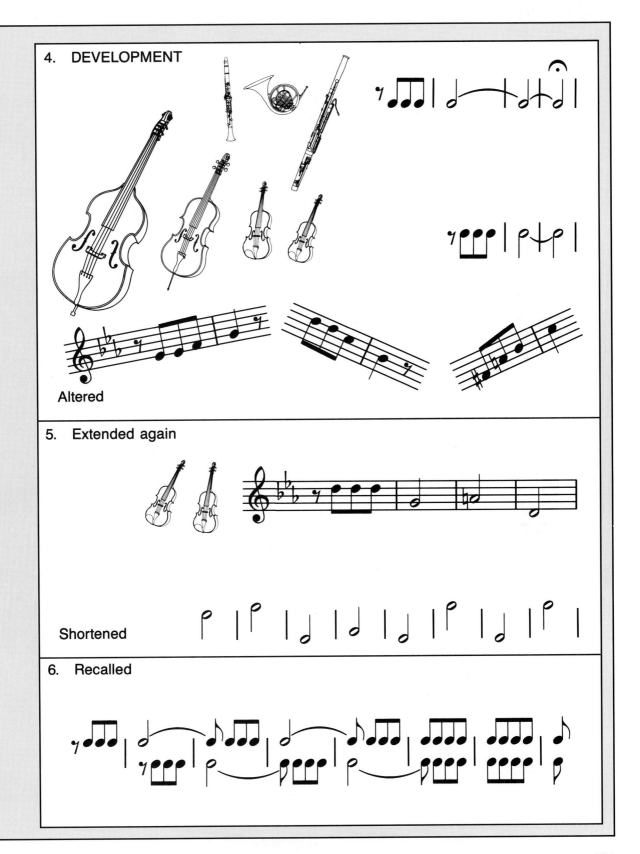

4. DEVELOPMENT

Altered

5. Extended again

Shortened

6. Recalled

## 7. RECAPITULATION

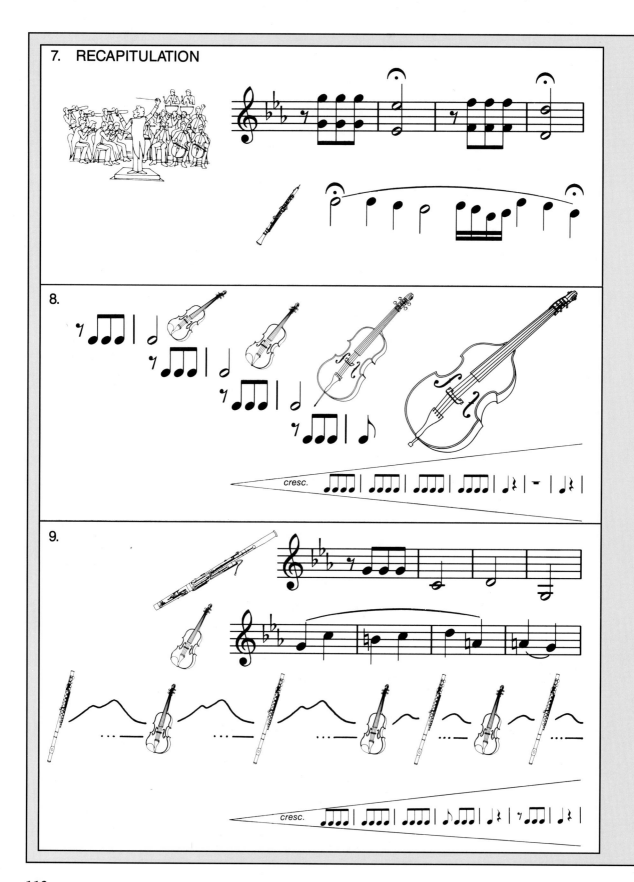

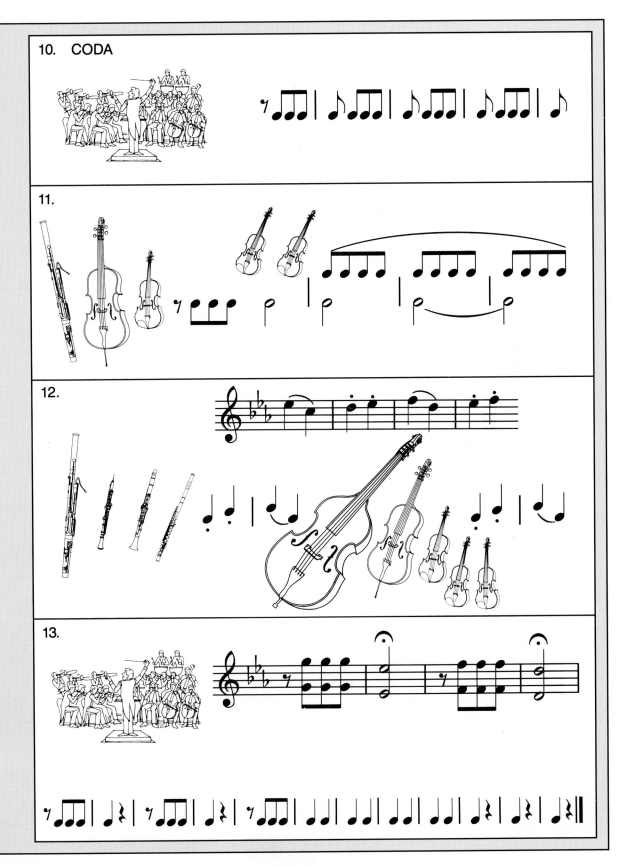

# No Man Is an Island

Words and Music by
Joan Whitney and Alex Kramer

Introduction

No man is an is-land, No man stands a-lone,

Each man's joy is joy to me, Each man's grief is my own.

We need one an-oth-er, So I will de-fend

(2nd time to Coda)

Each man as my broth-er, Each man as my friend.

freely

crescendo

I saw ___ the peo-ple gath-er, I heard ___ the mu-sic start,

The song — that they were sing-ing is ring-ing in my heart.

⊕ *Coda*    *ff*

friend, — Each man is my friend. _____

## LISTENING

# Prelude

### from *L'Arlésienne, Suite No. 1*

by Georges Bizet

Here is the main theme of the first movement from a suite by Bizet. Can you determine its form by examining the notation?

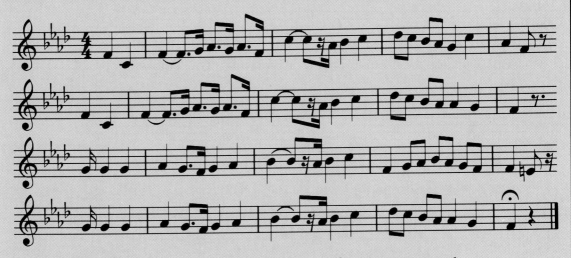

Listen to the complete composition. Do you find new musical ideas? Is the main theme repeated? varied? How many sections do you hear?

Create your own musical map of this composition. Use a half of a sheet of paper for each section. In each box put pictures of the instruments you hear playing the most important melody or accompaniment. Add terms that describe the tempo and the dynamics. Are there other things you notice that you can describe with words or pictures?

# Aye, Aye, Aye-Aye (The Limerick Song)

Traditional

Apply your knowledge of form, rhythm, and melody to learn this song.

*Refrain*

**F**  **A7**  **B♭**

Aye,  aye,  aye - aye, _____

**C7**  **F**

In  Tex - as  they  claim they grow  big - ger, _____

**F**  **C7**

So  tell me an - oth-er  that's  worse than the  t'oth-er,

**C7**  **F**  *Fine*

And  dust  it  all  o - ver with  sug - ar. _____

*Verse*  **F**  **C7**

1.  A  tu - tor who  toot-ed the  flute, _____
2. There  was  a  young  lad - y named  Wright, _____
3. There  was _ a  din - er named  Drew, _____

**C7**  **F**

Tried to  tu - tor two  toot-ers to  toot, _____
Who _  trav-eled much fast - er than  light. _____
Who _  found an old  shoe in his  stew. _____

116

The minuet is a dance which was popular during the Revolutionary War period. Many composers used the minuet form as part of compositions written to be performed in the concert hall. This minuet is part of a suite written by Wolfgang Amadeus Mozart over two hundred years ago.

Learn the minuet dance steps. You can perform it with this symphonic minuet even though Mozart did not intend it to be danced. The minuet is performed in sets of four couples.

The basic minuet step is $\frac{3}{4}$ ♩ ♩ ♩ | ♩. |
step  step  step      point

Do this pattern during the Minuet sections:

Move forward with three minuet steps.

Face your partner; bow or curtsy; turn around.

Do this pattern during the Trio sections:

Face your partner and "balance"; do this motion twice.

Exchange places by moving around your partner with six walking steps.

Bow or curtsy to your partner.

# Swing Low, Sweet Chariot

Spiritual
Arranged by William S. Haynie

*Refrain*

Swing low, sweet char - i - ot, __ Com-ing for to car-ry me home,

*Fine*

Swing __ low, sweet char - i - ot, __ Com-ing for to car-ry me home.

*Verse*

1. I looked o - ver Jor - dan and what did I see? __
2. If you get __ there __ be - fore __ I do, __
3. I'm some-times __ up __ and some - times down, __

Com-ing for to car - ry me home.
{ A band __ of an - gels
{ Just tell __ my friends I'm
{ But still __ my soul feels

*D.C. al Fine*

com-ing af - ter me, __
com - ing __ too, __   } Com-ing for to car-ry me home.
heav - en - ly __ bound, __

120

**Add these parts to "Swing Low, Sweet Chariot":**

1.

Swing   low   char - i - ot

2.

Swing   low,   swing   low,

3.

All   night,   all _____ day,

An - gels   watch - ing   o - ver   me,   My   Lord, __

All   night,   all _____ day,

An - gels   watch - ing   o - ver   me.

# The Bells of St. Mary's

Words by Douglas Furber

Music by A. Emmett Adams

Demonstrate your ability to hear and describe

# FORM *Rhythm* *Melody* HARMONY

Close your books. Listen to "The Bells of St. Mary's."

- First, listen for the **form**. Describe it with letters.
- Second, listen for the **rhythm**. Show it with "musical plus signs."
- Third, listen for the **melody**. Write it with scale numbers.
- Finally, listen for the **harmony**. Can you hear when the chords change?

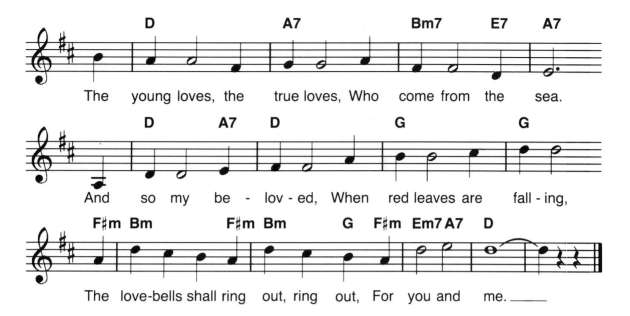

**D**        **A7**        **Bm7**    **E7**    **A7**

The young loves, the true loves, Who come from the sea.

**D**    **A7**    **D**        **G**        **G**

And so my be - lov - ed, When red leaves are fall - ing,

**F♯m Bm**      **F♯m Bm**     **G**   **F♯m Em7 A7**   **D**

The love-bells shall ring out, ring out, For you and me. ____

- Form a bell choir. Each member will play one bell.
- Add a chordal accompaniment.
- Check the pitches that make up each chord to determine when each member should play.

I      II7      IIM7      III      IV      V7      VI(7)

*The South Ledges, Appledore* (detail), 1913, by Childe Hassam.
Oil on canvas. Smithsonian Institution, Washington, D.C.

# Who Will Buy?

Words and Music by Lionel Bart

Who will buy this won-der-ful morn - ing?

Such a sky you nev-er did see. ____

Who will tie it up with a rib - bon,

And put it in a box for me? ____

1. So I can see it at my lei - sure ____
2. There'll nev - er be a day so sun - ny, ____

From the Columbia Pictures-Romulus film OLIVER!
©Copyright 1960 and 1968 Lakeview Music Co. Ltd., London, England
TRO—Hollis Music, Inc., New York, controls all publication rights for
the U.S.A. and Canada Used by Permission

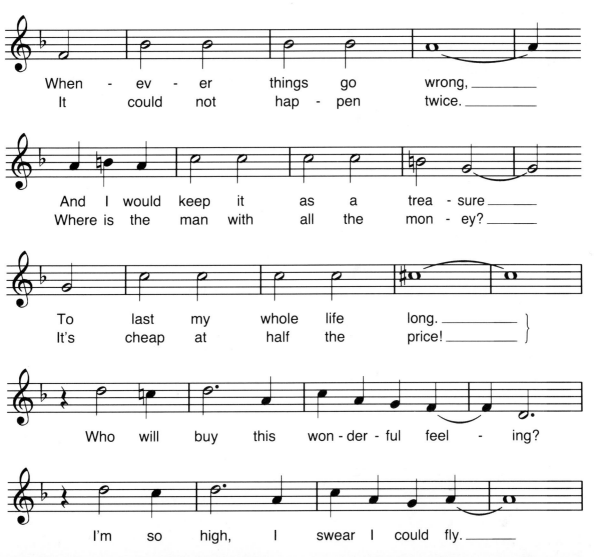

When - ev - er things go wrong, _____
It could not hap - pen twice. _____

And I would keep it as a trea - sure _____
Where is the man with all the mon - ey? _____

To last my whole life long. _____ ⎫
It's cheap at half the price! _____ ⎭

Who will buy this won - der - ful feel - ing?

I'm so high, I swear I could fly. _____

125

Me, oh, my, I don't want to lose ____ it,

So what am I to do, to keep the sky so blue?

1.
There must be some-one who will buy. ____

2.
buy. ____

# A Day in the Life of . . .

Everyone has feelings! Feelings change as situations happen. We experience many different feelings in a single day.

As a class, create a composition entitled "A Day in the Life of . . ." What will need to be done?

- Develop a story line in which the main character experiences different emotions. What will happen to the main character? Will it be realistic or make-believe? Determine four or five separate scenes.
- Divide into groups. Each group will choose one of the scenes. One group will be responsible for "threading" the scenes together with a theme song.
- Write the lyrics of the theme song. Compose the melody. Determine the scale to be used, and what accompaniment is needed. Devise a way of notating the music so it can be remembered.
- Practice individual scenes. Combine the scenes. Insert the song between each.
- Enjoy the performance!

# Freedom

Words by Peter Udell

Music by Gary Geld

**With energy**

Free - dom!

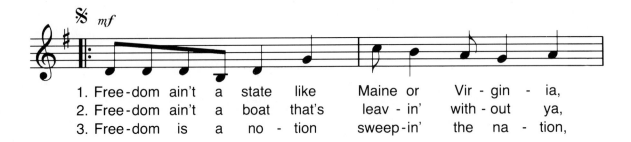

1. Free-dom ain't a state like Maine or Vir - gin - ia,
2. Free-dom ain't a boat that's leav - in' with - out ya,
3. Free-dom is a no - tion sweep-in' the na - tion,

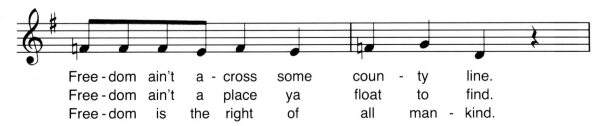

Free - dom ain't a - cross some coun - ty line.
Free - dom ain't a place ya float to find.
Free - dom is the right of all man - kind.

Free - dom is a flame that burns with - in ya,
Free - dom is the how ya think a - bout ya,
Free - dom is a bod - y's 'mag - i - na - tion,

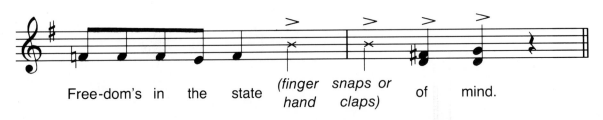

Free-dom's in the state *(finger snaps or hand claps)* of mind.

*From Shenandoah,* Lyric by Peter Udell and Music by Gary Geld
© 1974, 1975, GARY GELD and PETER UDELL.
All Rights Controlled by EDWIN H. MORRIS & COMPANY, A Division of MPL Communications, Inc.
International Copyright Secured  All Rights Reserved  Used by Permission

Refrain

Free - dom,     free - dom.     Free-dom,     free - dom.

3rd time to Coda

Free-dom is a flame that     burns with-in ya.     Free-dom's in the state _

1.
(Clap or stomp)     of mind.     2. of mind.     You   can't get to free-dom by

rid - in' on a     train. _____     The     on-ly way to free-dom is

D.S. al Coda

right   on through your     brain. _____     Wo-wo - wo - wo-wo.

Coda

of     mind!     Free - dom!

129

# Shenandoah

by Peter Udell and Gary Geld

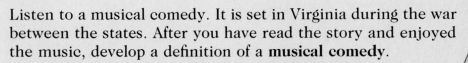

Listen to a musical comedy. It is set in Virginia during the war between the states. After you have read the story and enjoyed the music, develop a definition of a **musical comedy**.

**Scene 1:** The family is gathered around the breakfast table. They begin to discuss the Civil War, which has just begun. An argument arises between the father, who is opposed to any involvement in the war, and his sons, who believe that they should protect their home state of Virginia.

## I've Heard It All Before

**Scene 2:** Charlie and his family arrive late for church and interrupt the service. They take their places in the front pew, and the minister resumes his sermon. Many of the men have already left to fight, so there are more women than men in the congregation. The minister preaches on the duty that the people owe their state and directs his remarks to Charlie because his sons are all still at home.

**Scene 3:** After church, a group of Confederate soldiers enter the Anderson farmyard, looking for water. The officer asks Charlie why his sons have not joined the Confederate army, and Charlie angrily replies that his sons belong to him and not to the state. The officer becomes angry and reaches for his rifle, but not before all six of the sons have the soldiers covered. The soldiers leave, and the boys are awed by the feeling of power. Instead of putting down their guns, they sing "Next to Lovin' (I Like Fightin' Best)," ending with a dance.

## Next to Lovin' (I Like Fightin' Best)

**Scene 4:** The officer and his men are found dead on Charlie's land, probably killed by Yankee soldiers. Charlie is still not willing to send his sons to the army. He visits his wife's grave to think the matter through.

**Scene 5:** In spite of the fact that the war is going on, Jenny decides to marry Sam, who is about to go off to join the Confederate Army. As Jenny's sister-in-law Anne helps her get ready for the wedding, they sing "We Make a Beautiful Pair."

## We Make a Beautiful Pair

**Scene 6:** Later, as part of the wedding ceremony, Jenny and Sam sing about how beautiful their life will be together in the song "Violets and Silverbells." (Turn to pages 134–135 and follow the notation for this song as you listen to the recording.)

## Violets and Silverbells

**Scene 7:** The war, and the argument between the North and the South about freedom for the slaves, are difficult for the younger members of the family to understand. Anne tries to explain freedom to Robert and his friend, Gabriel, as they sing "Freedom." (Turn back to pages 128–129 and follow the words.)

## Freedom

**Scene 8:** Charlie's youngest son, Robert, is kidnapped by the Yankee soldiers because they saw him wearing a rebel cap and thought he was an enemy soldier. The Anderson family is shocked, outraged, and frightened. Charlie feels especially bad since this is his youngest son. Charlie decides that now they must get involved in the war. He and the others leave the farm to search for Robert. They are still searching when the war ends. Charlie and his family stop trains heading north, free the prisoners, and then burn the trains in an effort to find Robert and to show their anger at the Yankees for their treatment of the boy.

The freed soldiers are looking forward only to returning home. A corporal and his men sing of their longing.

## The Only Home I Know

**Scene 9:** Charlie and his family return home, still not having found the youngest son. They go to church. As the congregation is singing, Robert, ragged and dirty, comes limping in. All are excited and filled with joy as Charlie and his youngest son are reunited.

The musical comedy ends with the entire cast on stage singing "Freedom." Turn back to page 128 and sing the song to end this performance.

# Violets and Silverbells

Words by Peter Udell

Music by Gary Geld

Vi - 'lets 'n' sil - ver bells, grapes on the vine,

Love, like a vine-yard grows del - i - cate wine.

Sug - ar 'n' cin - na-mon, pep - per 'n' spice;

Love is the rec - i - pe that fla - vors a life.

Sure as the bri - ar and bram - ble en - twine,

Voice 1

So will it al - ways be your dreams and mine.

Voice 2

So will it al - ways be your dreams and mine.

Dai - sies and mar - i - gold, ro - ses that climb, __

Dai - sies and mar - i - gold, ro - ses that climb, __

Love, like a gar-den grows sweet - er with time. ____

Love, like a gar-den grows sweet - er with time. ____

So will our gar-den grow sweet - er with time. ____

So will our gar-den grow sweet - er with time. ____

# The Lady in the Harbor

Words and Music by Therese McGrath Meyer

Not just the wretch - ed and home - less,

Not just the poor and a - fraid,

But teach-ers, farm-ers, doc-tors, build-ers, oth-ers by the score,

Bring - ing with them a skill or a trade.

Not just the tired and the wear - y,

The ea - ger and strong sailed by my feet.

The po - et, the dream - er, the sing - er and his songs,

The dar - ing march - ing to a dif - ferent beat.

I stand _____ look-ing out 'cross the o - cean,

I stand _____ look-ing o - ver the sea,

And I hear ___ from the shore-line a cho - rus

call-ing to those ___ who long to be free.

A torch ___ shin-ing out through the dark - ness,

A light ___ to con-quer all fear,

And the call ___ from A-mer - i - ca thun - der-ing

That free - dom is wait - ing here.

The free-dom to speak, to ar-gue, to dif - fer ___

The right to come, to go, ac-cept or re - fuse.

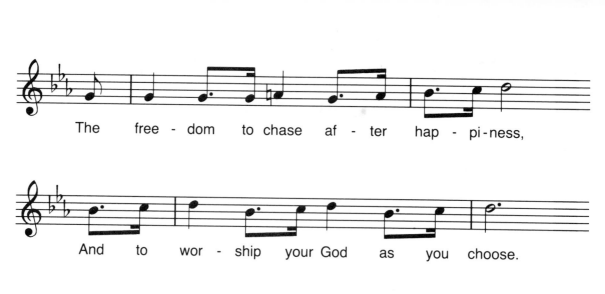

The free - dom to chase af - ter hap - pi - ness,

And to wor - ship your God as you choose.

I stand _____ in the storm and the thun - der,

I stand _____ though the sun burns and sears.

I wait _____ as I have for a cen - tu - ry, _____

_____ For you who hold on - to dreams I will hold out new hope.

I will hold up my lamp through all the com - ing years. _____

# Review 4

## Sinner Man

Traditional Folk Spiritual

Oh, sin - ner man, where you gon - na run to?

Oh, sin - ner man, where you gon - na run to?

Oh, sin - ner man, where you gon - na run to,

All on that day?

### Chromatic Scale Ruler

| C | C#/Db | D | D#/Eb | E | F | F#/Gb | G | G#/Ab | A | A#/Bb | B | C | C#/Db | D | D#/Eb | E | F | F#/Gb | G | G#/Ab | A | A#/Bb | B | C |
|---|---|---|---|---|---|---|---|---|---|---|---|---|---|---|---|---|---|---|---|---|---|---|---|---|

What scale is used for "Sinner Man"?

- Look at the ending pitch.
- Check the key signature.
- Use the Scale Ruler.

# Ifca's Castle

Traditional Round

1. 2.
A - bove the plain of gold and green,

3. 4.
A young boy's head is plain - ly seen;

5. 6.
A hu - ya, hu - ya, hu - ya - ya, Swift-ly flow-ing riv - er,

7. 8.
A hu - ya, hu - ya, hu - ya - ya, Swift-ly flow-ing riv - er.

# Unit 2

# More Music To Explore

# Perform Music

Learn to perform "Ama Lama." Work in small groups. One group should learn the melody on resonator bells.

A second group should learn to play a harmonizing part on the recorder.

A third group may add an accompaniment on the guitar.

## Ama Lama

Traditional
Arranged by Maureen Kenney

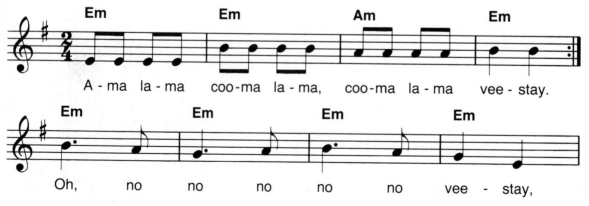

A - ma la - ma coo - ma la - ma, coo - ma la - ma vee - stay.

Oh, no no no no no vee - stay,

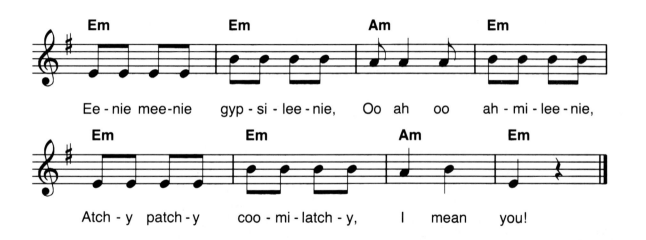

Ee - nie mee-nie  gyp - si - lee - nie,  Oo  ah  oo  ah - mi - lee - nie,

Atch - y  patch - y  coo - mi - latch - y,  I  mean  you!

# Playing the Recorder

## Explore Sounds

- While blowing gently, cover different combinations of holes.

## Play Pitches

- Cover the thumb hole and the finger hole nearest the mouthpiece.
- Add a finger to cover the next hole.
- Add another finger over the next hole.
- Play these familiar melodies:
  "Hot Cross Buns"
  "Rain, Rain Go Away"

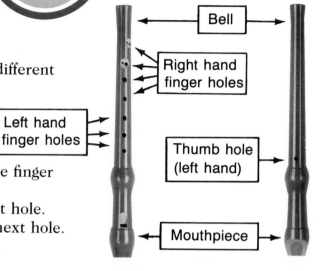

FRONT VIEW          BACK VIEW

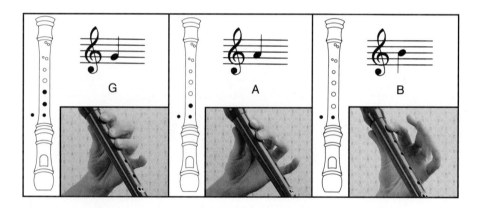

G          A          B

# Babylon's Fallin'

Virginia Folk Song

Ba - by - lon's   fall - in',   fall - in',   fall - in',

Ba - by - lon's   fall - in'   to   rise   no   more.

# The Rattle Sna-wa-wake

American Folk Song

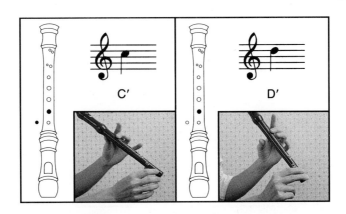

1. A nice young ma - wa - wan Lived on the hi - wi - will;
2. He scarce had mo - wo - wowed Half 'round the fie - we - wield
3. "O Pap - py Da - wa - wad, Go tell my ga - wa - wal

A nice young ma - wa - wan, For I knew him we - we - well.
'Til a rat - tle sna - wa - wake Bit him on the he - we - weel.
That I'm goin' to di - wi - wie, For I know I sha - wa - wall."

*Refrain*

To my rat - tle, to my roo - rah - ree.

4. "Oh John, O Joh-wa-wahn,
   Why did you go-wo-wo
   Way down in the mea-we-dow
   So far to mo-wo-wo?"
   *Refrain*

5. "Oh Sal, O Sa-wa-wal,
   Why don't you kno-wo-wow
   When the grass gets ri-wi-wipe
   It must be mo-wo-wowed?"
   *Refrain*

6. Come all young gir-wi-wirls
   And shed a tea-we-wear
   For this young ma-wa-wan
   That died right he-we-were.
   *Refrain*

7. Come all young me-we-wen
   And warning ta-wa-wake,
   And don't get bi-wi-wit
   By a rattle sna-wa-wake.
   *Refrain*

147

# Lonesome Traveler

Words and Music by Lee Hays

Here are two new pitches. Which one of them uses a "forked" fingering?

**Rhythmically**

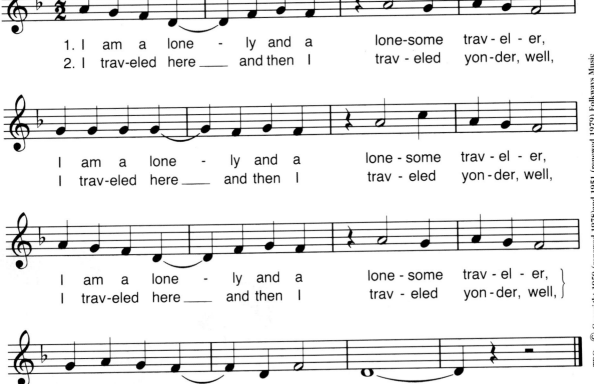

1. I am a lone - ly and a lone-some trav - el - er,
2. I trav-eled here ___ and then I trav - eled yon-der, well,

I am a lone - ly and a lone - some trav - el - er,
I trav-eled here ___ and then I trav - eled yon-der, well,

I am a lone - ly and a lone - some trav - el - er,
I trav-eled here ___ and then I trav - eled yon-der, well,

I've been a trav - el - in' on. ___

# The Hippopotamus

Music by Jean Berger

Play a melody that uses two "forked" fingerings.

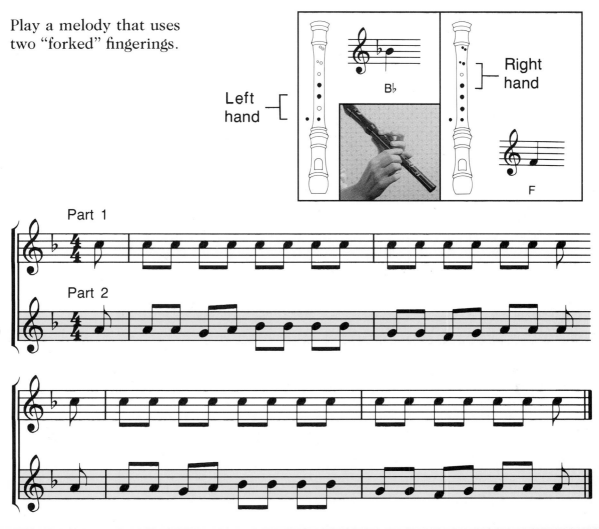

# The John B.'s Sails

Calypso

So hoist up the John B.'s sail. See how the main-sail's set.

Send for the cap-tain a - shore, let me go home.

Let me go home, let me go home.

I feel so break up; let me go home.

# Wanderin'

American Folk Song

Practice the fingerings for C and E. Then play "Wanderin'."

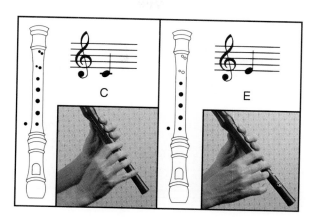

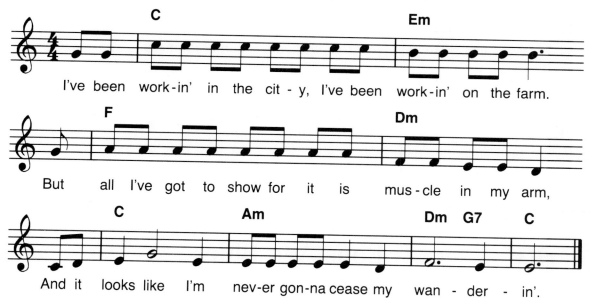

I've been work-in' in the cit - y, I've been work-in' on the farm.

But all I've got to show for it is mus-cle in my arm,

And it looks like I'm nev-er gon-na cease my wan - der - in'.

## Music of the Spheres

### by Lord Byron

There's music in the sighing of a reed;
There's music in the gushing of a rill;
There's music in all things, if men had ears;
Their earth is but an echo of the spheres.

- Form groups.
- Create a setting of this poem using recorders and percussion instruments.

# Walkin' Blues

Words and Music by B. A.

Learn to play "Walkin' Blues" on your recorder. Remember . . .
you must blow gently to produce the low tones.

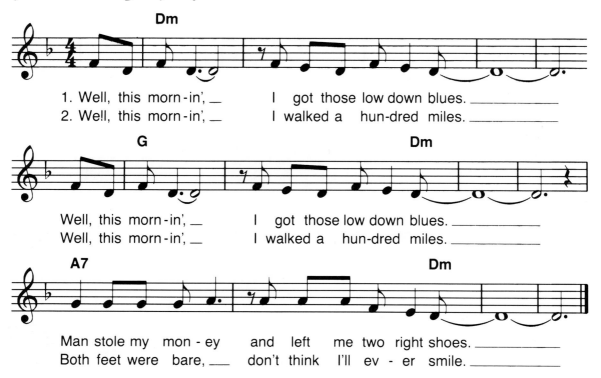

1. Well, this morn-in', — I got those low down blues. _____
2. Well, this morn-in', — I walked a hun-dred miles. _____

Well, this morn-in', — I got those low down blues. _____
Well, this morn-in', — I walked a hun-dred miles. _____

Man stole my mon-ey and left me two right shoes. _____
Both feet were bare, ___ don't think I'll ev-er smile. _____

## LISTENING

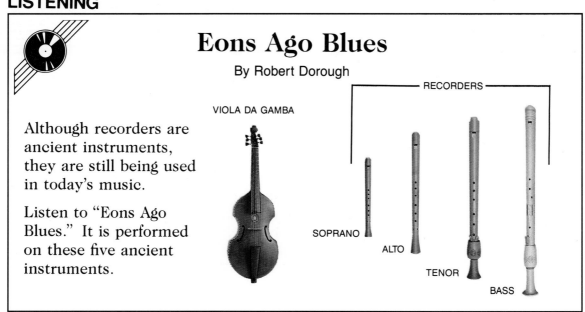

# Eons Ago Blues

By Robert Dorough

Although recorders are ancient instruments, they are still being used in today's music.

Listen to "Eons Ago Blues." It is performed on these five ancient instruments.

VIOLA DA GAMBA

RECORDERS

SOPRANO

ALTO

TENOR

BASS

# Three to Get Ready

by Dave Brubeck

# Minuet in G

Learn to perform Section A of this composition on bells and bass xylophone. Work in pairs.

Play the **treble clef** part on resonator bells. Which bells will you need?

Play the **bass clef** part on the bass xylophone. Can you identify the letter names of the pitches you will need by reading the bass clef?

D   F♯   G   A   B   C   D

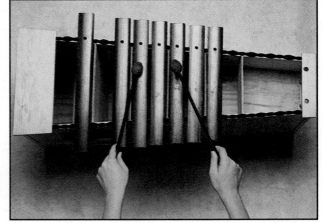

by J. S. Bach

# To a Wild Rose

1. "Ch"
2. "Doo"
3. "Doo"

**With simple tenderness** (♩=88)

from *Woodland Sketches*
by Edward MacDowell

♩ means to tap the bell lightly and rapidly to sustain
the sound.

# Dance of the Sugarplum Fairy

from *Nutcracker Suite*
by Peter Ilyich Tchaikovsky
Arranged by Frederick Beckman

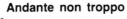

158

**Andante non troppo**

Bell 3

- Identify each part of your guitar.

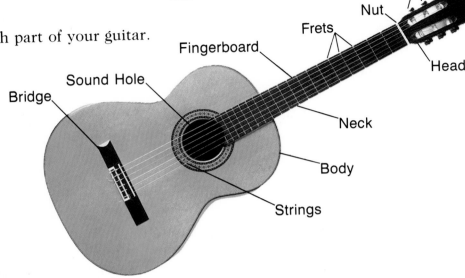

Tuning Pegs
Nut
Frets
Fingerboard
Head
Sound Hole
Bridge
Neck
Body
Strings

- Learn to hold your guitar so there are four points of contact with your body:
  1. underneath the right forearm;
  2. against the chest;
  3. inside the right thigh;
  4. on the left knee.

- Examine the diagrams to learn where to place your fingers for two chords.

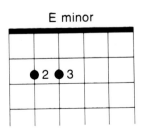

E minor

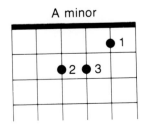

A minor

# Me and My Captain

Traditional

Review the melody (page 28). Then accompany yourselves using only the E minor chord. Strum on the first and third beats.

Me and my captain don't agree,
But he don't know 'cause he don't know me.
He don't know, he don't know my mind,
When he sees me laughin',
Just laughin' to keep from cryin'.

# Chicka-Hanka

Track Laborer's Song

Accompany this song using E minor and A minor chords. Strum on the first and third beats.

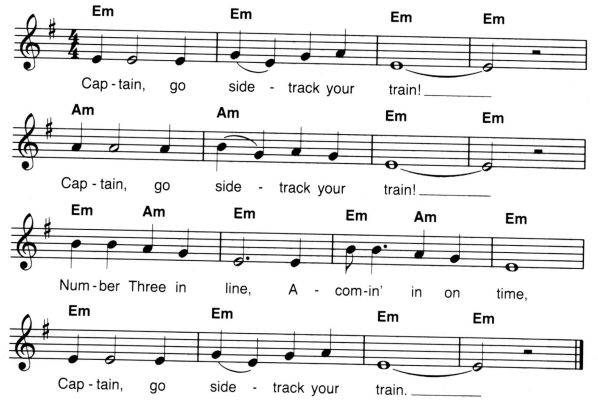

Cap - tain, go side - track your train! _____

Cap - tain, go side - track your train! _____

Num - ber Three in line, A - com-in' in on time,

Cap - tain, go side - track your train. _____

161

# Johnny Has Gone for a Soldier

American Folk Song

Can you determine the scale on which this song is based?

Can you find patterns based on any of these chords in this song?

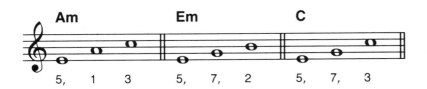

Practice the patterns. Then sing the melody.

162

Vocal chording accompaniment:

Group 1:  Sing the melody with words.

Group 2:

Group 3:

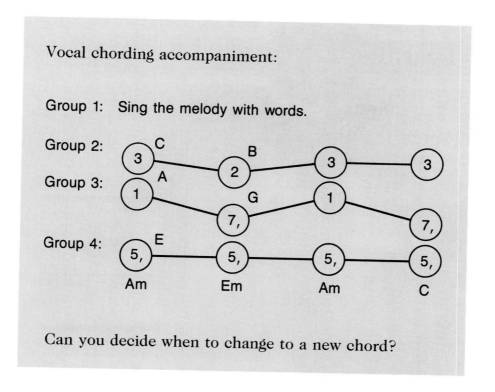

Group 4:

Can you decide when to change to a new chord?

You will need to play these chords:

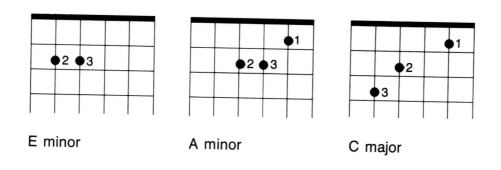

E minor          A minor          C major

Practice this chord sequence:

$\frac{4}{4}$ Am / / / | Em / / / | Am / / / | C / Am / |

Am / Em / | Am / / / | C / / / | Am / / / ||

# Learning a New Chord

Use the C chord to accompany songs you know:

"Row, Row, Row Your Boat"

"Frère Jacques"

Learn the G7 chord. When you can play the G7 chord, practice changing between C and G7. Play this chord sequence:

# He's Got the Whole World in His Hands

Spiritual

Use C and G7 chords to accompany this song.

**C**

1. He's got the whole world _ in His hands, _
2. He's got _ you and me broth - er, in His hands, _
3. He's got the lit - tle bit-ty ba - by in His hands, _
4. He's got _ ev - ery-bod-y here _ in His hands, _

**G7**

He's got the whole world _ in His hands, _
He's got _ you and me sis - ter, in His hands, _
He's got the lit - tle bit-ty ba - by in His hands, _
He's got _ ev - ery-bod-y here _ in His hands, _

**C**

He's got the whole world _ in His hands, _
He's got _ you and me broth - er, in His hands, _
He's got the lit - tle bit-ty ba - by in His hands, _
He's got _ ev - ery-bod-y here _ in His hands, _

**G7**            **C**

He's got the whole world in His hands. _____

165

# Describe Music

How well can you describe what you hear?

Can you describe the way rhythms and melodies move?

Within a piece of music, can you identify the small parts that make up the larger sections?

Can you describe how the small parts and larger sections combine to make an interesting piece of music?

# Accentuate the Positive

Words by Johnny Mercer

Music by Harold Arlen

Listen to the song on this page. Describe everything you can
about the music. Demonstrate by singing the song that being
able to describe music helps you learn how to perform it.

You've got to accentuate the positive,
Eliminate the negative,
Latch on to the affirmative,
Don't mess with Mister In-between.

You've got to spread joy up to the maximum,
Bring gloom down to the minimum,
Have faith or pandemonium
Li'ble to walk upon the scene.

To illustrate . . . my last remark,
Jonah in the whale, Noah in the Ark,
What did they do just when everything
    looked so dark?

"Man," they said,
"We better accentuate the positive,
Eliminate the negative,
Latch on to the affirmative,
Don't mess with Mister In-between."
No! Don't mess with Mister In-between.

# When I'm on My Journey

Traditional Black American Song

How well can you describe the song by looking at this picture of the music? Can you describe the melody and rhythm? Can you describe the form?

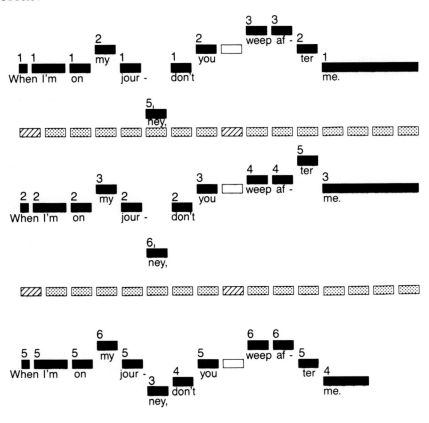

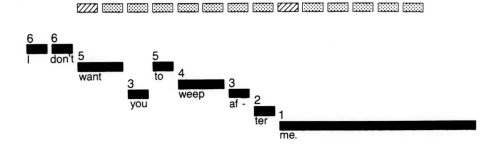

This is a harmony part to be sung as an accompaniment to "When I'm on My Journey." Can you describe how it will sound?

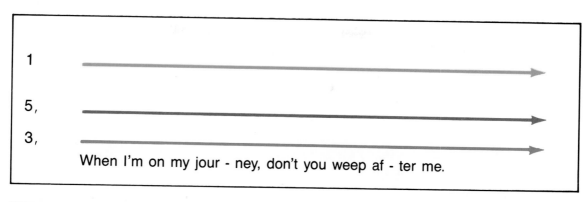

1

5,

3,

When I'm on my jour - ney, don't you weep af - ter me.

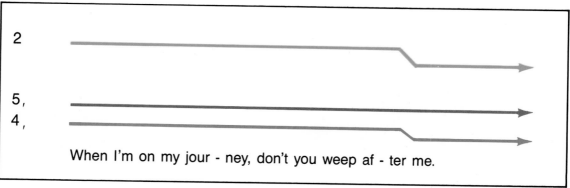

2

5,

4,

When I'm on my jour - ney, don't you weep af - ter me.

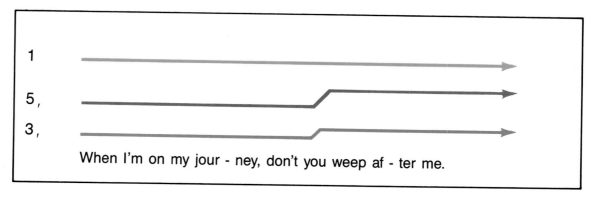

1

5,

3,

When I'm on my jour - ney, don't you weep af - ter me.

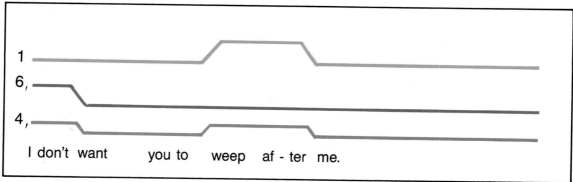

1

6,

4,

I don't want     you to     weep  af - ter  me.

# Raindrops Keep Fallin' on My Head

Words by Hal David

Music by Burt Bacharach

**Moderato, rhythmically**

Rain - drops keep fall - ing on my head,

And just like the guy whose feet are too big for his bed,

Noth - in' seems to fit. Those rain - drops are fall - in' on my head.

They keep fall - in', so I just did me some talk - in' to the sun,

And I said I did-n't like the way he got things done.

Sleep-in' on the job. Those rain-drops are fall-in' on my head.

They keep fall-in'! But there's one thing I know, ____

The blues ____ they send ____ to meet ____ me won't de-feat ____ me.

It won't be long ____ till hap-pi-ness ____ steps up ____ to greet ____ me. ____

Rain-drops keep fall-in' on my head,

But that does-n't mean my eyes will soon be turn-in' red.

Cry-in's not for me, 'cause I'm nev-er gon-na stop the rain by com-plain-in'.

Be-cause I'm free, noth-in's wor-ry-in' me. ____

# The Counting Game

Music by Grant Beglarian

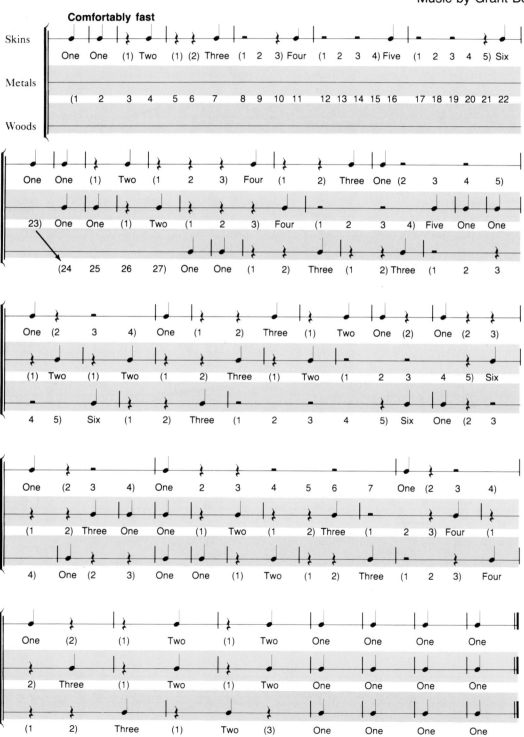

# Trinidad

Words and Music by
Massie Patterson and Sammy Heyward

1. Joe was just___ a young is - land lad, ___ and his
2. Joe, he bought_ all her wed - ding clothes,_ but this
3. Trin - i - dad, ___ she was ver - y cute, ___ and they

girl-friend named_ Trin - i - dad, She would not an - swer a
was the start___ of his woes; He bought a dress_ made of
said she was ___ quite a beaut, But she said she ___ did not

yes or no, ___ this young girl from Puer - to Ri - co.
fine sat - in, ___ but now where's the love - ly Lat - in?
care to wed,_ her heart was in San_ Juan in - stead.

*Refrain*

Trin - i - dad,_ oh, Trin - i - dad, _ please, my dar - ling, don't

act so mean. _ Please come back ___ to me;

ain't it plain _ to see, I will make_ you my queen.

# Everybody Loves Saturday Night

African Folk Song

To read a new song, you need to know the scale on which it is based. As you learn the songs on this page and the next, go through the steps listed below. Determine the scale on which each song is based.

- Find the tonal center of the melody, often the final tone.
- Starting with that pitch, circle all the different pitches in the song on a Chromatic Scale Ruler.
- Put the Major and Natural Minor Scale Finders over the Chromatic Scale Ruler. Which one matches the pattern of whole and half steps created by the circled pitches?

1.

Ev-ery-bod - y       loves   Sat-ur-day    night. _____
*Mo -fe  mo - ni     s'mo     ho __ gbe - ke.* _____

2.

Ev-ery-bod - y       loves   Sat-ur-day    night. _____
*Mo -fe  mo - ni     s'mo     ho __ gbe - ke.* _____

3.

Ev-ery-bod-y,        ev-ery-bod-y,        ev-ery-bod-y,        ev-ery-bod-y,
*Mo-fe mo-ni,        mo-fe mo-ni,        mo-fe mo-ni,        mo-fe mo-ni,*

4.

Ev - ery - bod - y   loves   Sat-ur-day    night. _____
*Mo - fe  mo - ni     s'mo     ho __ gbe - ke.* _____

174

# Shalom Alëhem

Jewish Folk Song

Follow the same steps to discover the scale of this song.

Hë - vë - nu sha - lom a - lë - hem,

Hë - vë - nu sha - lom a - lë - hem,

Hë - vë - nu sha - lom a - lë - hem,

Hë - vë - nu sha - lom, sha - lom, sha - lom a - lë - hem.

175

# The Owlet

English Words Adapted

Mexican Folk Song

Different versions of this lullaby are sung by Spanish-Americans in the Southwest. Learn to sing the melody and harmonizing part of this arrangement.

Andantino

**F**
Te - co - lo - te, lit - tle owl - et, _____

**Gm** ti - ny bird of the ear - ly **C** morn, _____

**F**
Won't you lend to me your wing - lets _____

**C7** so that I may go to my **F** love? _____

**Bb**
Won't you lend me your lit - tle wing - lets, _____

**F**
won't you lend me your lit - tle wing - lets, _____

**Gm** won't you lend me your lit - tle **C7** wing - lets _____

so that I may go to my love?

Te - cu - ru - cú y cú y cú,

te - cu - ru - cú y cú y cú.

Po - bre - ci - to te - co - lo - te.

You are too tired _ to cry now. Te - cu - ru - cry. _____

177

# As the Sun Goes Down

Words and Music by Josef Marais

Many songs combine passages that move by scale steps with passages that are based on chordal tones. In this song, most of the patterns are drawn from these three chords.

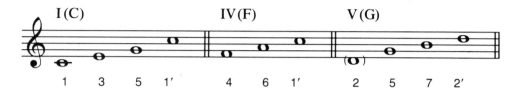

Put a clear sheet of plastic over the musical notation of the song. Locate patterns based on these three chords. Circle each chordal pattern with a different color.

Locate patterns that seem to be based on scale steps. Circle these with a fourth color.

Did you find the notes in the scale patterns that pass between two tones of a chord? These are called **passing tones.**

Practice singing the song as you play the chords. First sing on "loo" or with numbers. Then sing the words.

1. I think of my dar - ling as the sun goes down,
2. I'll see my dear dar - ling as the sun comes up,

The sun goes down, the sun goes down;
The sun comes up, the sun comes up;

I think of my dar - ling as the sun goes down,
I'll see my dear dar - ling as the sun comes up,

178

*Fine*

Down,    down be - low    the    moun - tain.
Up,    up    a - bove    the    moun - tain.

*Refrain*

I'll    ride, I'll ride, I'll ride, I'll ride, I'll    ride    all    night,

When the    moon    is    bright,    when the    moon    is    bright;

I'll    ride, I'll ride, I'll ride, I'll ride, I'll    ride    all    night,

*D.C. al Fine*

I'll    get    there    in    the    morn - ing.

179

# Oh, Give Me the Hills

Miner's Song

**With motion**

1. Oh give me the hills and the ring of the drills
3. Oh give me the hills in a far west-ern land

and the rich sil - ver ore in the ground, _____
for I'm home - sick when - ev - er I roam; _____

Where sel - dom is heard a dis - cour - a - ging word
I'll dig for the ore in the hills to be found

And man - y true friends will be found. _____
In the land that I love to call home. _____

2. Oh give me a land where a man __ may stand
3. Oh give me the hills in a far west-ern land,

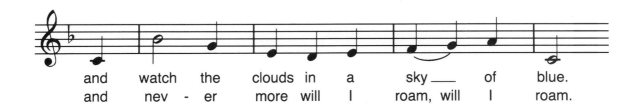

and watch the clouds in a sky __ of blue.
and nev - er more will I roam, will I roam.

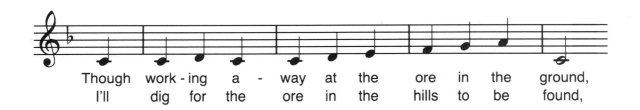

Though work-ing a - way at the ore in the ground,
I'll dig for the ore in the hills to be found,

his dreams may come true. _____
In the land I call home. _____

# A Spacey Suite

Words by Frederick Winsor

Music by Fred Willman

What makes a **suite?**

## 1.Little Miss Muffet

**Easy blues**

Lit - tle Miss Muf - fet _____ sits on her tuf - fet _____

In a non - cha - lant sort of way.

With her force field a - round her, the Spi - der, the bound - er,

Is not in the pic - ture to - day, O yeah! __

# 2.Little Bo Peep

**Gently**

Lit - tle Bo Peep has lost ___ her sheep, the ra - dar has failed to find them. They'll all face to face meet in par - al - lel space, pre - ced -ing their lead-ers be - hind ___ them.

# 3.Little Jack Horner

**Brightly**

Lit - tle Jack Hor - ner sits in a cor - ner Ex - tract - ing cube roots to in - fin - i - ty, An as - sign - ment for boys that will min - i - mize noise And pro - duce a more peace -ful vi - cin - i - ty.

# 4. Baby's Hi-Fi

Re - sis - tor, tran - sis - tor, con - dens-ers in pairs,

Re - sis - tor, tran - sis - tor, con - dens-ers in pairs.

**I** Bat - ter - y, plat - ter, re - cord me some airs;

**II** Bat - ter - y, plat - ter, re -

Squeak-er and squawk-er and woof - er times *pi*, And ba - by shall have his own

cord me some airs; Squeak-er and squawk-er and woof - er times *pi*, And

pri - vate hi - fi. _____

ba - by shall have his own pri - vate hi - fi.

# 5.In the Beginning of the End

**Very slowly**

Sing   a song   of sau - cers   flown   from out - er space,

Four   and twen - ty gen - er - als   crim - son   in   the face.

The   sau - cers con - quered grav - i - ty   so   they   all be-gan   to spin,

And   gen -tle-men,   if   you'll par - don me, ____ this   is where I came   in.

*Faster (blues tempo)*

# First Suite in E♭

by Gustav Holst

Play these pitches. How did the composer use them?

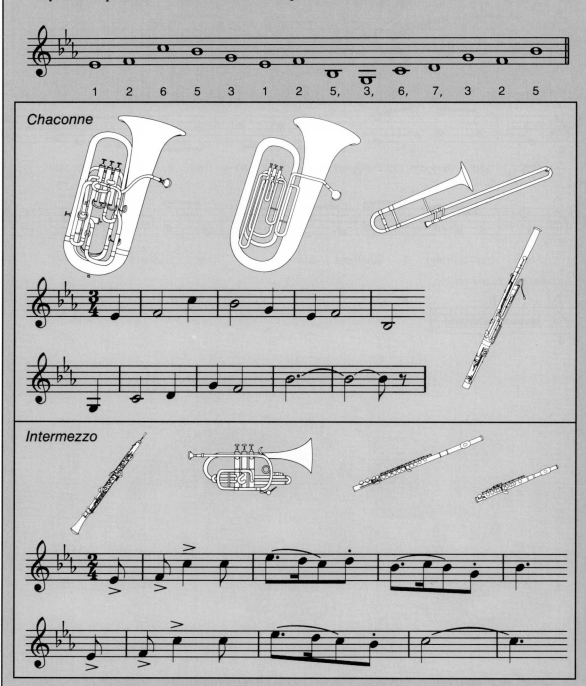

Chaconne

Intermezzo

# Cloudburst

## from *Grand Canyon Suite*

### by Ferde Grofé

Ferde Grofé composed music to describe his impressions of the Grand Canyon. The final movement describes a cloudburst.

1. The music begins with a melody that suggests the beauty of the canyon and the glorious colors of the sunset.

2. Cellos warn that all may not be peaceful!

   Winds and percussion join.

3. The storm builds.

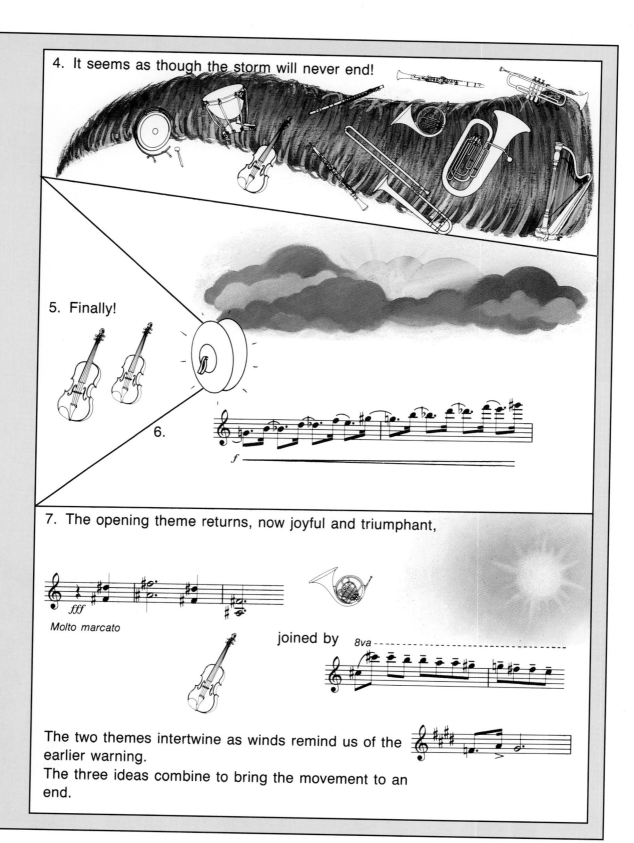

4. It seems as though the storm will never end!

5. Finally!

6.

*f*

7. The opening theme returns, now joyful and triumphant,

*fff*

*Molto marcato*

joined by

*8va* - - - - - - - - - - - - - - - - - - - -

The two themes intertwine as winds remind us of the earlier warning.

The three ideas combine to bring the movement to an end.

# Create Music

Improvise melodies that make musical sense.

**1.**

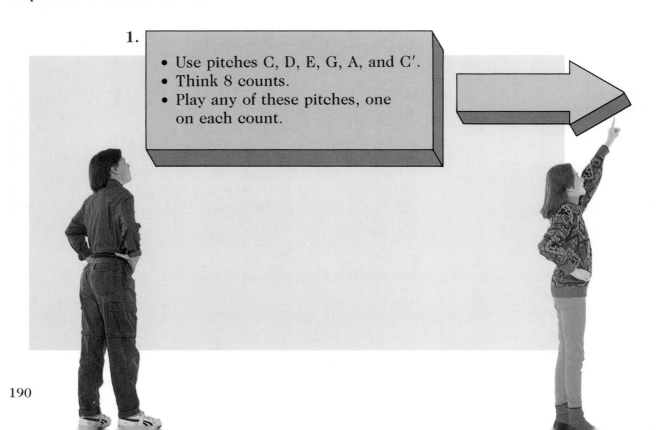

- Use pitches C, D, E, G, A, and C′.
- Think 8 counts.
- Play any of these pitches, one on each count.

**2.**
- Think phrases with 8 counts.
- Play on counts 1 through 7; rest on 8.
- The final pitch played must be a C.
- Play several sets of these 8-count phrases.

**3.**
- Think phrases of 8 counts.
- First phrase: you must end on C.
- Second phrase: do not end on C.

**4.**
- Explore phrases that move with a feeling of 3s.
- Feel the phrase in 12 counts.
- Count and play on counts 1–10; rest on 11 and 12.
- Add accents on counts 1, 4, 7, and 10.

**5.**
- Play a question phrase (do not end on C).
- Play an answer phrase (must end on C).

**6.**
- Divide one count into two short sounds.
- Choose the count on which you will divide the beat.

**7.**
- Use a phrase length of 8 or 12 counts.
- Create a phrase that you can easily repeat.
- Play two phrases that are the same, one that is different, then repeat the original phrase.

**8.**
- Make up tunes that suggest cowboy or merry-go-round music.
- What in the music will "trigger" these ideas? Rhythm? Melody? Harmony? All of these elements?

# Greensleeves

Old English Folk Song

Listen to "Greensleeves" as it might have been performed when it was first written, nearly 500 years ago.

1. A - las! my love, you do me wrong,
2. Ah, Green - sleeves, now fare - well, a - dieu,

To cast me off dis - cour - teous - ly;
To God I pray to pros - per thee,

For I have loved you, oh, so long,
For I am still thy sweet - heart true;

De - light - ing in your com - pa - ny.
Come once a - gain to meet me.

*Refrain*

Green - sleeves was all my joy, And oh, Green - sleeves was my de - light.

Green-sleeves,__my heart of gold,__And all __ for La - dy Green-sleeves.

**LISTENING**

# Fantasia on "Greensleeves"

by Ralph Vaughan Williams

## Greensleeves

by The Ramsey Lewis Trio

When you play an instrument, you must make the same kinds of musical decisions as when you sing. You must decide how you are going to "shape" each musical phrase through changes in

# ACCENT   TONE QUALITY
# DYNAMICS   *Tempo*   ARTICULATION

Listen to *Fantasia on "Greensleeves"* in a setting for string orchestra. Notice how the instrumentalists play this melody in a simple "singing" style. As you listen, determine where each phrase reaches its high point.

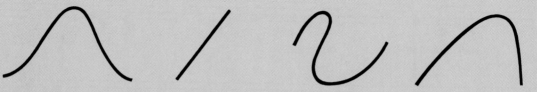

How do the performers use different musical controls to shape the phrases?

Compare this setting with an interpretation of "Greensleeves" by a jazz group, the Ramsey Lewis Trio. What differences do you notice in the way the phrases are shaped?

# Greensleeves in Modern Dress

Arranged by Buryl Red

Listen to a recording session in which a rock combo develops a
1960s rock version of this traditional melody.

Sing the song in this new meter.

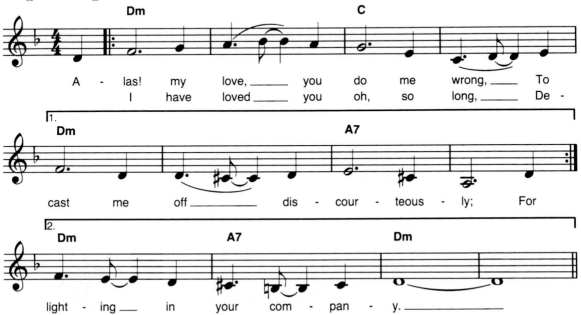

A - las! my love, _____ you do me wrong, _____ To
I have loved _____ you oh, so long, _____ De -

1. cast me off _____ dis - cour - teous - ly; For

2. light - ing _____ in your com - pan - y. _____

Harmony: Add vocal "fills" during long tones in the melody.

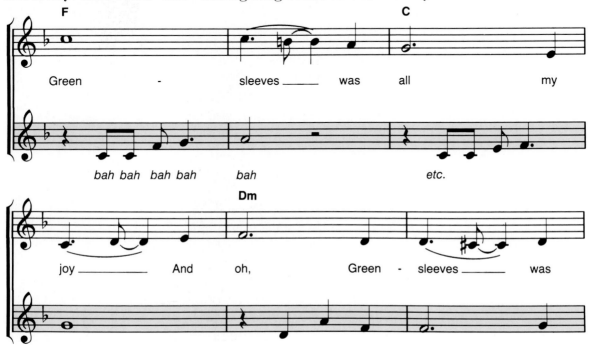

Green - sleeves _____ was all my

*bah bah bah bah    bah*                          *etc.*

joy _____ And oh, Green - sleeves _____ was

my de - light. Green -

sleeves, _____ my heart of gold, _____ And

all _____ for La - dy Green - sleeves.

Create your own arrangement. Will you perform this song in the style in which it was performed hundreds of years ago? Or would you do it in a sixties folk-rock arrangement?

# Four to Make a Melody

Play these musical phrases in sequence to create a comedy chase arrangement.

## Shades of Sennett

Music by Henry Mancini

196

Create a contrasting melody.

Pitches for improvisation are supplied in the boxes.

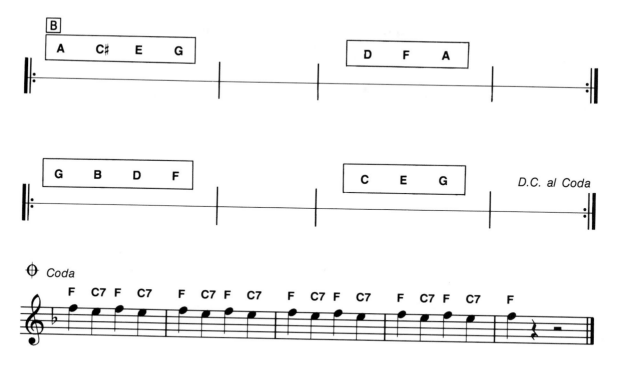

| B | | | |
|---|---|---|---|
| A | C# | E | G |

| D | F | A |
|---|---|---|

| G | B | D | F |
|---|---|---|---|

| C | E | G |
|---|---|---|

*D.C. al Coda*

Coda

F  C7  F  C7   F  C7  F  C7   F  C7  F  C7   F  C7  F  C7   F

## LISTENING

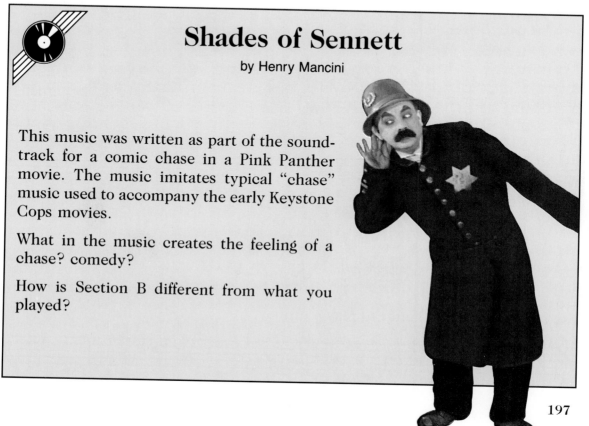

# Shades of Sennett

by Henry Mancini

This music was written as part of the sound-track for a comic chase in a Pink Panther movie. The music imitates typical "chase" music used to accompany the early Keystone Cops movies.

What in the music creates the feeling of a chase? comedy?

How is Section B different from what you played?

197

# Creating Eastern Indian Music

Classical Indian music is one of the oldest forms of music in the world, dating back nearly 2,000 years. Learn about this music.

There are four main elements in Indian music: drone, melody, rhythm, and improvisation.

A drone instrument (tambura)

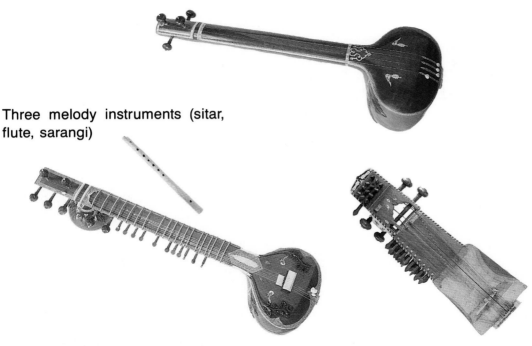

Three melody instruments (sitar, flute, sarangi)

Two rhythm instruments (tabla, or pair of drums)

Use a specially tuned guitar to play a drone:

# Play a Raga

A **raga** is a group of pitches rather like a melody. Each raga has its own particular mood. Each raga is meant to create a mental picture or image. Different ragas are played at different times of day: morning, noon, evening, and night. Some ragas express happiness, courage, or humor, while others express sorrow, peace, or even anger.

Every raga has a special ascending and descending scale. The musician can improvise only on these tones.

Play each of the following ragas. Compare the quality of each.

**Morning raga** (*Vibhas*)
Mood: loveliness; sound of the early dawn

**Afternoon raga** (*Bilavad*)
Mood: pleasant and joyful

**Evening raga** (*Marwa*)
Mood: restless and uncomfortable

**Night raga** (*Malakosh*)
Mood: peaceful and meditative

Choose one set of pitches. Improvise music in the mood of that raga while others accompany with a drone.

199

# Play a Tala

**Tala** means "clap." It is also thought of as a "rhythmic cycle." The most commonly played tala, called *Tintal*, has 16 beats. The strongest beats in this tala are the 1st, 5th, and 13th beats.

```
X               X               0               X
1   2   3   4   5   6   7   8   9   10  11  12  13  14  15  16
```

The *x* represents the strong beats (which are clapped) and the *o* means a weak or silent beat (usually expressed by a wave of the hand).

Clap or use percussion instruments to play another tala. This one has 4 beats instead of 16. Avoid loud instruments such as the big drum or large cymbals. Sticks, woodblocks, castanets, bells, bongos, or any kind of small drum can be used.

Divide into four groups. Group 1 counts out the tala with the claps. Groups 2, 3, and 4 play their parts on suitable instruments.

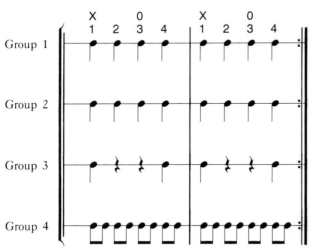

Add this tala to one of the ragas you played on page 199.

- Begin with the drone.
- Add the raga.
- Add the tala.
- Improvise on the raga.

200

# Improvisation on a Raga

Each raga has four important pitches. These four pitches have to be emphasized at certain sections of the performance.

1. The *vadi* or King—the pitch that is most often repeated
2. The *samvadi* or Chief Minister—follows the King everywhere
3. The *anuvadi* or Servant
4. The *vivadi* or Enemy—causes discord or clashes with the other sounds

Here are some characters in a raga. Can you identify who they are?

**LISTENING**

# Tenderness

### by Ravi Shankar

Notice that the drone is heard first. A slow statement of the raga is presented. The tabla enters with the drone accompaniment. The melody returns at a faster tempo. The musicians continue the piece, improvising on the raga and tabla, gradually increasing the tempo until ending with a dramatic climax.

# Patriotic Polymelodies

## We the people of...

Ask not what your country...   Give me liberty or give me...

Fourscore and seven years ago...

We the people of...

Divide into four groups. Perform "Patriotic Polymelodies."

Group 1: "America"              Group 2: "America the Beautiful"
Group 3: "Yankee Doodle"        Group 4: "Battle Hymn of the Republic"

Put it all together.

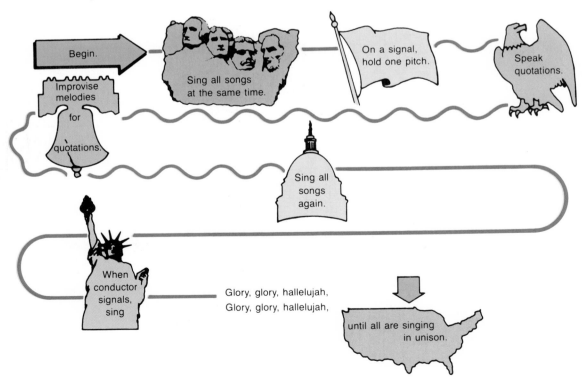

Begin.

Improvise melodies for quotations.

Sing all songs at the same time.

On a signal, hold one pitch.

Speak quotations.

Sing all songs again.

When conductor signals, sing

Glory, glory, hallelujah,
Glory, glory, hallelujah,

until all are singing in unison.

# Borrowed Melodies

The following parts of melodies have been reported as missing. Learn to sing each example. Then solve the mystery of the borrowed melodies.

Exhibit A—missing from Handel's "Messiah"

Hal - le - lu - jah!

Exhibit B—missing from "Bring Back My Bonnie to Me"

Oh bring back my Bon-nie to me!

Exhibit C—missing from "Bohemian Girl," by Balfe

I dreamt_ I dwelt_ in mar - ble halls,

I had rich - es too great to count. _____

Exhibit D—missing from "An Old-Fashioned Garden"

It's just an old fash - ioned gar - den _____

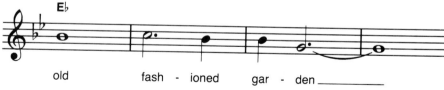

old fash - ioned gar - den _____

The Prime Suspect: Song "Yes! We Have No Bananas."
All Points Bulletin: Last seen at the top of the 1923 Hit Parade.
Assignment: Check it out. Determine: guilty or not.

# Yes! We Have No Bananas

Words and Music by
Frank Silver and Irving Cohn

We have an old-fash-ioned to-mah-to,_____

Long Is-land po-tah-to._____

But Yes! We have no ba-na-nas,_____

We have no ba-na-nas to-day._____

Sing this song using the original composers' words. What is the one new musical idea in the song?

Create a "borrowed" tune. Combine phrases from songs in the book to create a new melody. The tune should make "some musical sense." Think about phrase lengths, rhythm, melody, and harmony. See if your classmates can discover how you "created" your melody!

# The Rose

Words and Music by Amanda McBroom

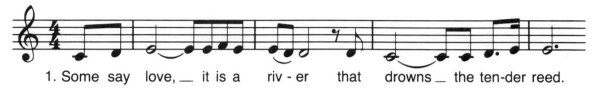

1. Some say love, — it is a riv-er that drowns — the ten-der reed.

Some say— love, — it is a ra-zor — that leaves — the heart to bleed.

Some say— love, — it is a hun-ger, an end-less ach-ing need. —

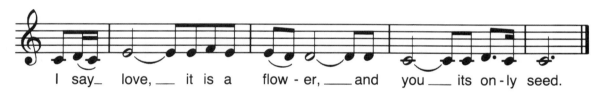

I say— love, — it is a flow-er, — and you — its on-ly seed.

2. It's the heart afraid of breaking,
    that never learns to dance.
   It's the dream afraid of waking,
    that never takes the chance.
   It's the one who won't be taken,
    who cannot seem to give,
   And the soul afraid of dying,
    that never learns to live.

3. When the night has been too lonely,
    and the road has been too long,
   And you think that love is only
    for the lucky and the strong,
   Just remember in the Winter,
    far beneath the winter snow,
   Lies the seed that with the sun's love,
    in the Spring becomes the Rose.

Play this melody:

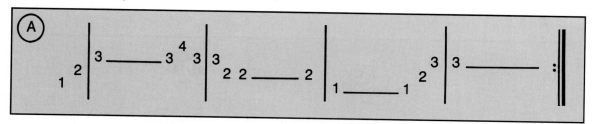

Add an accompaniment.

First, play once for each chord change as shown in the box below.

Next, create your own rhythmic ideas, still following the sequence of chord changes. Use your ideas to accompany the melody.

Chord Changes:

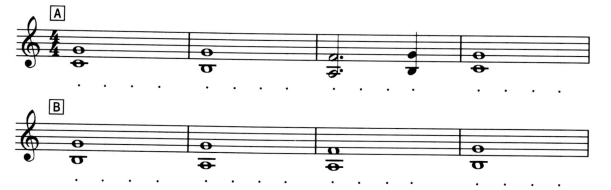

# Special Times

## Cindy

Traditional
Arranged by Max T. Ervin

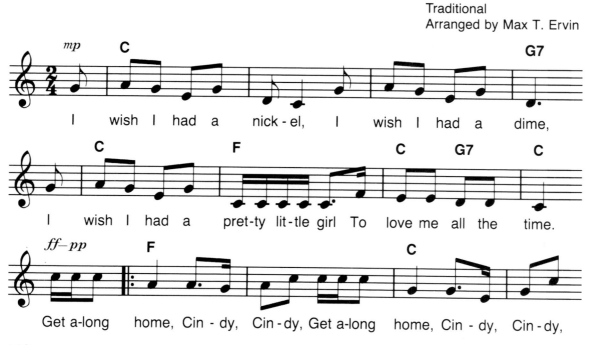

I wish I had a nick-el, I wish I had a dime,

I wish I had a pret-ty lit-tle girl To love me all the time.

Get a-long home, Cin-dy, Cin-dy, Get a-long home, Cin-dy, Cin-dy,

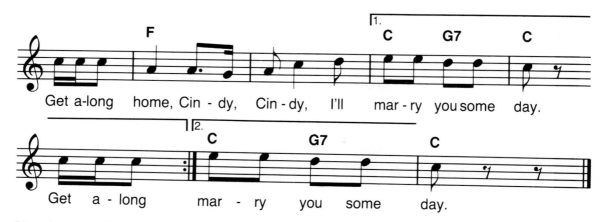

Get a-long home, Cin - dy, Cin - dy, I'll mar - ry you some day.

Get a - long mar - ry you some day.

You have a shouting voice, a whispering voice, and several different speaking voices for conversation, for giving speeches, and for giving orders.

Your singing voice can also be used in many different ways:

- rounds and canons
- **descants** and harmonies
- choral music

Use your singing voice to learn this **countermelody** for "Cindy."

I wish I had a nick - el, I wish I had a dime,

I wish I had a pret-ty lit-tle girl, love me all the time.

Go on home, my Cin - dy, Go on home, my Cin - dy,

Go on home, my Cin - dy, Mar - ry you some day.

Get a - long Mar - ry you some day.

# The Bells in the Steeple

Translation and Music by Carl Orff

The bells in the stee - ple

The bells in the stee - ple

The bells in the stee - ple

The bells in the stee - ple

1.     2.     3.     4.

The bells in the stee - ple ring out to the peo - ple,

"A storm's in the air. Take care! Be - ware!" —

Bim bim bim bim bam, bim bim bim bam,

bim bam, bim bam, bim bam, bim bam.

210

# A Swallow Song

Words and Music by Richard Fariña

Use your musical skills to learn this song. Learn the rhythm and the melody.

1. Come wan - der qui - et - ly and lis - ten to the wind.
2. There is no sor - row like the mur - mur of their wings,

Come near and lis - ten to the sky. _____
There is no choir __ like their song. _____

Come walk - ing high a - bove the roll - ing of the sea
There is no pow - er like the free - dom of their flight, __

And watch the swal - lows as they fly.
__ While the swal - lows roam a - lone.

When a performer has learned the melody and rhythm of a song, there are still many musical decisions to make. Can you think of some of the decisions a performer needs to make in order to perform a song expressively?

211

# You Are My Sunshine

Words and Music by Jimmy Davis

You are my sun - shine, \_\_\_ my on - ly sun - shine, \_\_\_

You make me hap - py \_\_\_\_ when skies are gray, \_\_\_\_

You'll nev - er know, dear, \_\_\_ how much I love you, \_\_\_

Please don't take my sun - shine a - way. \_\_\_\_

While some sing the melody to "You Are My Sunshine," others
may add a "vocal chording" accompaniment.

5    You   are   my   sun  -  shine,        my   on - ly   sun  -  shine, ⟶

3    You   are   my   sun  -  shine,        my   on - ly   sun  -  shine, ⟶

1    You   are   my   sun  -  shine,        my   on - ly   sun  -  shine, ⟶

               hap  -  py       when skies are

5 You   make me                            gray, ⟶

               hap  -  py       when skies are

3 You   make me                            gray, ⟶

1 You   make me   hap  -  py       when skies are     gray, ⟶

               know,   dear,      how   much   I

5 You'll nev-er                         love     you, ⟶

               know,   dear,      how   much   I

3 You'll nev-er                         love     you, ⟶

1 You'll nev-er     know,   dear,      how   much   I   love you, ⟶

5     Please don't take      my    sun - shine    a  -  way.

                               sun - shine    a

3     Please don't take      my                     - way.

1     Please don't take      my                     - way.

                               sun - shine    a

213

# When the Saints Go Marching In

New Words by Paul Campbell

1. We are trav - 'ling in the foot - steps _____
2. Some _ say this world of trou - ble _____

of those who've _ gone be - fore, _____
is the on - ly _____ one we need, _____

But we'll all be re - u - nit - ed _____
But I'm wait - ing for that morn - ing _____

on a new and sun - lit shore. _____
when the new world is re - vealed. _____

Oh, when the Saints _____ go march-ing in, _____

Oh, when the Saints go _____ march - ing in, _____

Oh, Lord, I ____ want to be in that num - ber _____

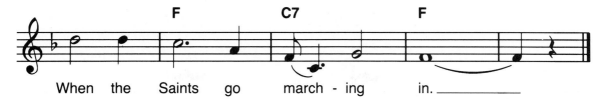

When the Saints go march - ing in. _____

Divide into groups. Use vocal chording to create four-part harmony for the refrain of the song.

5  Oh,  when the Saints    go  march - ing    in,
3  Oh,  when the Saints    go  march - ing    in,
1  Oh,  when the Saints    go  march - ing    in,

5  Oh,  when the Saints  go  march -    ing    in,
3  Oh,  when the Saints  go  march -    ing    in,
1  Oh,  when the Saints  go  march -    ing    in,

                                                 num - ber
5  Oh, Lord, I  want      to   be    in that  num - ber
4  Oh, Lord, I  want      to   be    in that  num - ber
7, Oh, Lord, I  want      to   be    in that  num - ber

6  When  the
               Saints  go      march - ing    in.
4  When  the
               Saints  go      march - ing    in.
1  When  the   Saints  go      march - ing    in.

215

# A New Setting for the Saints

Change the vocal accompaniment. Rhythmically **scat-sing** on
the pitches you have learned.

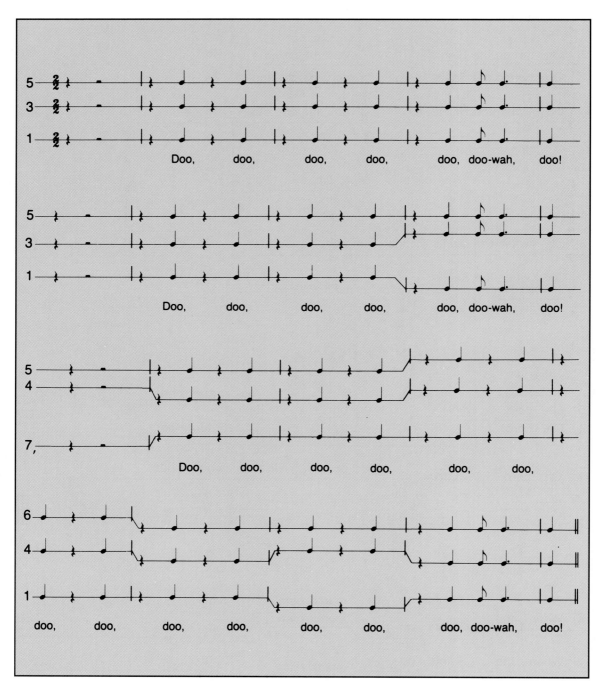

# The Keys of Heaven

English Folk Song

Moderately

Voice 1

F  Dm  Gm  C7  F  Gm  F  C7

1. I will give you the keys of ___ heav - en,
2. I will give you a blue silk ___ gown, ___
3. I will give you the keys to my heart, We'll

F  Dm  Gm  C7  F  Gm  F  C7

I will give you the keys of ___ heav - en,
Two stripes up and ___ three stripes _ down, ___
mar - ried be till ___ death do us part, ___

Voice 2

F  B♭  F  Gm  F  B♭  F  Gm

*Verses 1 & 2:* No, I will not walk! No, I will not
*Verse 3:* I will walk and talk! I will walk and

Voice 1

Mad-am, will you walk? Mad-am, will you talk?

F  Gm  F  Gm  F  C7  F

talk! No, no, I will not talk with thee.
talk! Yes, I will walk and talk with thee.

Mad - am, will you walk and talk with me?

# Sally, Don't You Grieve

Spiritual

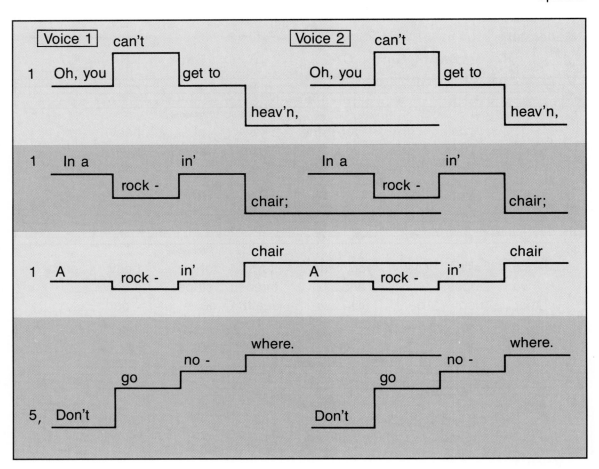

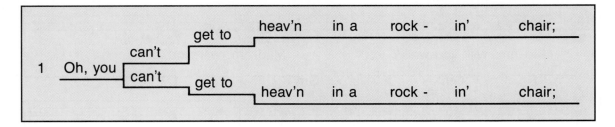

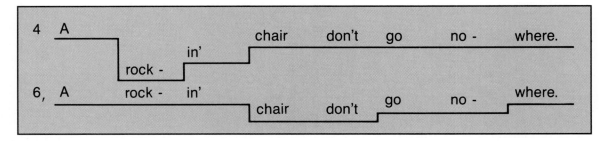

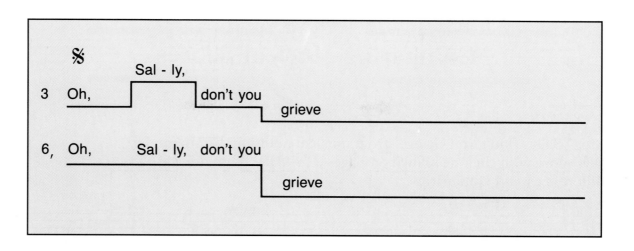

3  Oh,  Sal - ly,  don't you  grieve

6,  Oh,  Sal - ly,  don't you  grieve

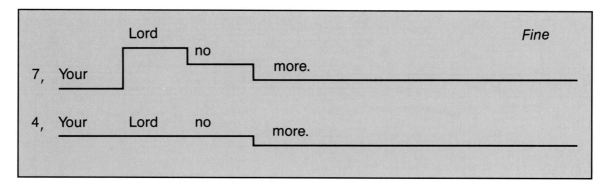

7,  Your  Lord  no  more.  *Fine*

4,  Your  Lord  no  more.

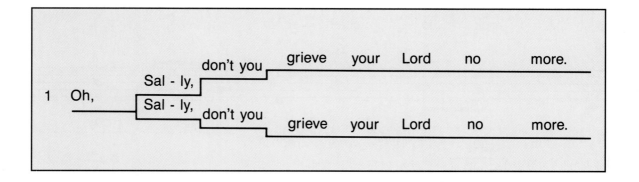

1  Oh,  Sal - ly,  don't you  grieve  your  Lord  no  more.
       Sal - ly,  don't you  grieve  your  Lord  no  more.

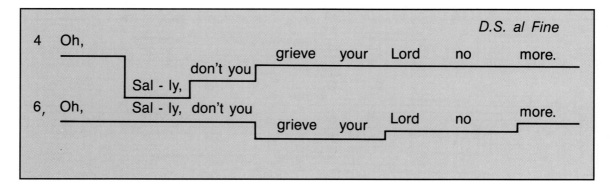

*D.S. al Fine*

4  Oh,  Sal - ly,  don't you  grieve  your  Lord  no  more.

6,  Oh,  Sal - ly,  don't you  grieve  your  Lord  no  more.

# Comparing Musical Scores

Sing "Sally, Don't You Grieve" from musical notation. Compare this score with the one shown on pages 218–219. What are the differences and similarities?

Oh, Sal - ly, don't you grieve _____ your Lord no more. _____

Oh, Sal - ly, don't you grieve your Lord no more.

Oh, Sal - ly, don't you grieve your Lord no more.

Oh, Sal - ly, don't you grieve _____ your Lord no more. _____

2. Oh, you can't go to heav'n on roller skates,
You'll roll right by those pearly gates.
Oh, you can't go to heav'n on roller skates,
You'll roll right by those pearly gates.

3. Oh, you can't get to heav'n in Dad's old car,
'Cause Dad's old car won't go that far.
Oh, you can't get to heav'n in Dad's old car,
'Cause Dad's old car won't go that far.

can't

1   Oh, you        get to

heav'n,

Oh, you can't get to heav'n

# The Bulldog

College Song
Arranged by B.A.

1. & 5. Oh, the bull-dog on the bank,
2. Oh, the bull-dog stooped to catch him,

And the bull-frog in the pool,
And the snap-per caught his paw.

Oh, the bull-dog on the bank, And the bull-frog in the pool,
Oh, the bull-dog stooped to catch him, And the snap-per caught his paw.

Oh, the bull-dog on the bank, And the bull-frog in the pool,
Oh, the bull-dog stooped to catch him, And the snap-per caught his paw.

The bull-dog called the bull-frog a green old wat-er fool.
The pol-ly-wog died a-laugh-in', to see him wag his jaw.

3. Says the monkey to the owl,
   "Oh, what'll you have to drink?"
   *(repeat twice)*
   "Why, since you are too very kind,
   I'll take a bottle of ink!"

4. Pharaoh's daughter on the bank,
   Little Moses in the pool;
   *(repeat twice)*
   She fish'd him out with a telegraph pole
   And sent him off to school!

Use bells or xylophones. Learn to play Section A of this song.

# The Country Party and Old Brass Wagon

American Folk Song
Arranged by Buryl Red

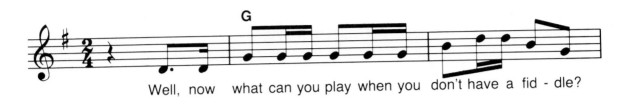

Well, now what can you play when you don't have a fid - dle?

Find a gui - tar with a hole in the mid - dle,

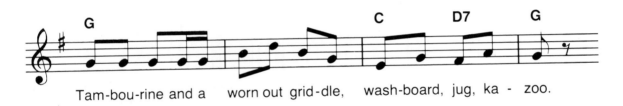

Tam-bou-rine and a worn out grid-dle, wash-board, jug, ka - zoo.

Oh! Cir - cle to the left, the old brass wag - on,

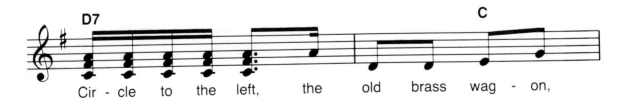

Cir - cle to the left, the old brass wag - on,

Cir-cle to the left, the old brass wag-on, you're the one, my dar - ling.

And what do you think we've got for sup - per?

Black - eyed peas and bread and but - ter,

Ducks in the duck-house all a - flut - ter, pick-led oys - ters, too!

Swing, oh swing,
Hey! the old brass wag - on,

Swing, oh swing,
the old brass wag - on,

Swing, oh swing, oh
the old brass wag-on, you're the one, my dar - ling.

You're the one, my (clap) dar - ling!

# Moonlight Bay

Words and Music by Edward Madden and Percy Wenrich

We were sail-ing a - long _____ on Moon-light

We were sail-ing a - long

Bay. _____ We could hear the voic - es ring - ing; _____

on Moon-light Bay.

ring - ing; _____

They seemed to say: _____ "You have stol-en my

They seemed to They seemed to say: _____

heart, _____ Now don't go 'way!" _____

___ "You have stol-en my heart, Now don't go 'way!"

As we sang love's old sweet song on Moon-light Bay (on Moon-light Bay).

As we sang love's old sweet song on Moon-light Bay (on Moon-light Bay).

## LISTENING

# Welcome Back to Dixieland
by Einar N. Pedersen

Listen to a modern barbershop quartet.

# Yesterday

Words and Music by Julie Barrier
Adapted and Arranged by Buryl Red

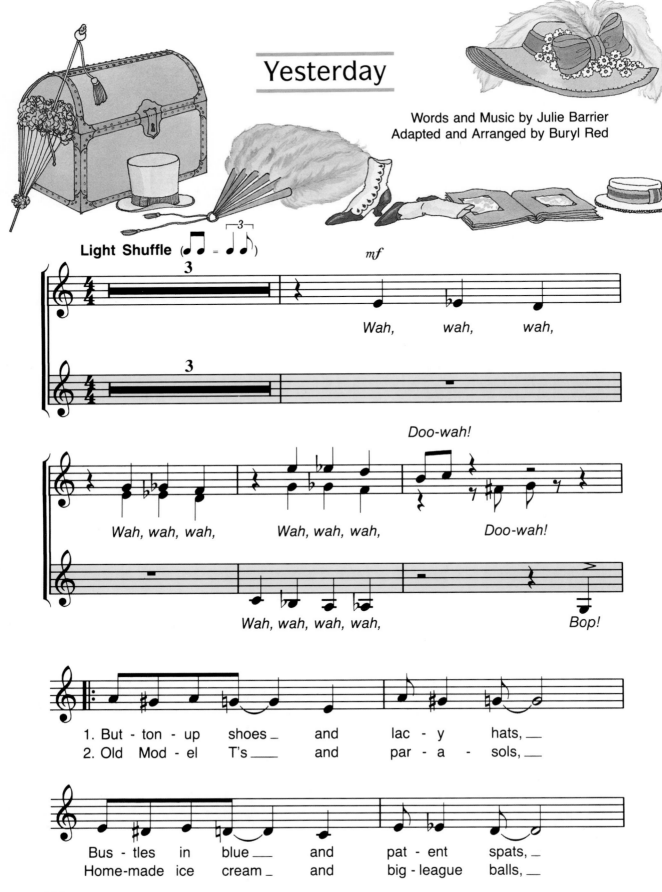

**Light Shuffle**

Wah, wah, wah,

Doo-wah!

Wah, wah, wah,    Wah, wah, wah,    Doo-wah!

Wah, wah, wah, wah,    Bop!

1. But - ton - up   shoes _   and    lac - y    hats, _
2. Old Mod - el   T's __   and    par - a - sols, _

Bus - tles   in   blue _   and    pat - ent   spats, _
Home-made  ice   cream _  and    big - league   balls, _

Gran - ny and Grand - pa __ walk in the park; __
Some-times I think __ I'd __ just love to hear __

No one's a - fraid __ to __ walk af - ter dark. __
What it was like __ in __ ear - li - er years. __

*Refrain*

Oh, yes - ter - day, __ Well, I've been think - in' 'bout

yes - ter - day! __ It's fun to dream a - bout

all of my rel - a - tives, born way back when. ___

Do I feel just __ the same as they did back then? __

I think of yes - ter - day, __ It's fun to dream a - bout

yes - ter - day! __ I love to find it out.

229

# Freedom

Words by Julie Barrier

Music by Buryl Red

**Jazz waltz feeling**

1. & 3. Run - ning with the breeze, look - ing to the sky.
2. Greet - ing a new day, smil - ing at the sun.

Go - ing where I please, reach - ing up so high.
Hap - py I can say I'm free to have fun.

Giv - en a chance to be me, _____

I've got to be all I can be to be free.

I can go where I want, do what I want,

Be what I want to be.

Play where I want, say what I want,

*3rd time, go to Coda*

All just be-cause I am free to be me.

Soar - ing like ea - gles who fly far a - way,

Mak - ing the most of each beau - ti - ful day,

232

# I Got Shoes

Spiritual
Arranged by Livingston Gearhart

Developing good breath control can help you sing more expressively. Breathe each time you see this mark ❜. Prepare your breathing so that you can sing each phrase in one breath. Be sure to control your breathing at the beginning so that you have some breath left at the end of the phrase.

walk
wear it } all    o - ver God's                   Heav-en, _____                    Heav-en, _____
sing it

*(suddenly soft)*
*pp*

Heav-en, _____                    Heav-en, _____

*(suddenly soft)*
*pp*

_____    Heav-en.      *Ah* _____

Heav-en, _____    Ev - ery-bod - y talk - in' 'bout   heav-en's not   go - in' there.

*mf*

Heav-en! _____    Heav-en!  { Gon - na    walk
                                Gon - na    wear it } all    o - ver God's
                                Gon - na    sing it

*mf*

Heav-en! _____    Heav-en! _____

| 1. & 2. | 3. |

Heav-en! _____    Heav-en!    *(Mmm)* _____

You can control the kind of sound you make when you sing.
This control is called **voice placement**.
To practice singing with a "bright" sound, hold your hand to the
bridge of your nose.
Sing this.

zing   zing   zing   zing   zing

Can you feel the vibrations in your nose? Now sing this.

zing   zing   zing   zing   zing          zing   zing   zing   zing   zing          etc.

To practice singing with a "dark" sound, imagine that you are
holding a hot potato in the back of your mouth. This will help
you open your throat. Now sing this.

hum _____          hum _____

## Sometimes I Feel Like a Motherless Child

American Folk Song
Arranged by Buryl Red

Practice singing with a dark sound; with a bright sound. Which
is more appropriate?

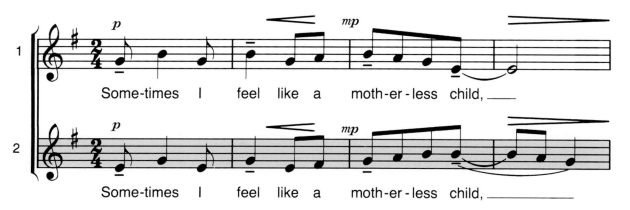

1  Some-times   I   feel   like   a   moth-er-less   child, _____

2  Some-times   I   feel   like   a   moth-er-less   child, _____

# Dixie

Words and Music by Dan Emmett
Arranged by Max T. Ervin

Oh, I wish I was in the land of cot - ton,

Oh, 'way down south, in Dix - ie,

Old times there are not for - got - ten, Look a - way!

There's a place that's not for - got - ten, Look a - way! down south

Look a - way! Look a - way! Dix - ie Land.

Hush my mouth, what a song, sing a - long,

In ___ Dix - ie Land _ where _ I was born in,

Dix - ie is where I was born,

Ear - ly on one frost - y morn-in', Look a - way!

Ear - ly on a frost - y morn-in', There was I,

Look a - way! Look a - way! Dix - ie Land.

Fresh as pie, Me - oh-my, My - oh-me,

Then I wish I was in Dix - ie, Hoo - ray! Hoo - ray!

Mis-sis-sip - pi, Lou'-si - an', South Car-o - li - na, Al - a-bam'.

In Dix-ie Land I'll take my stand to live and die in Dix-ie,

Dix - ie Land, live and die, Dix - ie Land,

A - way, a - way,

That's the place for me! There I want to be!

a - way down south in Dix - ie. A - way,

'Way down south in Dix - ie, That's the place for me!

a - way, a - way down south in Dix - ie.

There I want to be! 'Way down south in Dix - ie.

# Carmen, Carmela

Words Adapted

Mexican Folk Tune

The marimba and two violins that you hear on the recording
suggest an accompaniment you might hear in Mexico.

1. When day is done and the sun - set glows in the dis - tance,
2. And when the shad-ows are fall - ing, night birds are call - ing

light-ing a dusk - y sky, I wan - der back to the val - ley
as they de-scend in flight. The stars are glim-mer-ing bright-ly,

where my Car - me - la waits for my joy - ful cry.
clouds drift - ing light - ly, soft - ly we say, "good night."

*Refrain*

Car - men, Car - me - la, my gold - en sun - beam,

You ban - ish sor - row with one sweet smile.

May all good for - tune a - wait your plea - sure,

My gold - en trea - sure, Car - me - la, mine. _____

# Boogie-Woogie Ghost

Words and Music by Nadine M. Peglar

1. There was a ghost on Hal - low - een, He real - ly
2. He'd go out spook - ing late at night, And giv - ing

made the ghost - ie scene, He was the Boo - gie - Woo - gie Ghost, He was the
ev - ery-one a fright, He knew some wit - ches, two or three, And they would

ghost - ie with the most, And when the kid - dies came a - round, He'd give out
all go on a spree, And when the morn - ing came a - round, He'd give one

with a ghost-ly sound, He'd go, ___ "Boo - oo - oo - oo - ooo."
last mys-te - rious sound, He'd go, ___ "Boo - oo - oo - oo ooo."

Though he real - ly was - n't ver - y spook - y, _____

Kids all thought that he was rath - er cool.

E - ven though he was a lit - tle kook - y, _____

He was just a spe - cial _____ ghoul. When you're

out on Hal - low-een And he ap - pears up - on the scene, Don't give a

scream and run a - way, Just ask him if he'll stay and play. You'll like the

Boo - gie-Woo - gie Ghost, He'll be the one you dig the most, You'll love his

Boo - oo - oo - oo - ooo.

## LISTENING

# Bru's Boogie-Woogie

### by Dave Brubeck

Listen for this pattern. Which notes does the bass play?

# Prayer of Thanksgiving

Words Translated by Theodore Baker

Netherlands Folk Song
Arranged by Edward Kremser

1. We gath-er to-geth-er to ask the Lord's bless-ing,
2. Be - side us to guide us, our God with us join - ing,
3. We all do ex - tol thee, thou lead - er tri - um - phant,

He chas - tens and has - tens his will to make known;
Or - dain - ing, main - tain - ing his king - dom di - vine,
And pray that thou still our de - fend - er will be.

The wick - ed op - press-ing now cease __ from dis - tress-ing.
So from the be - gin - ning the fight ___ we were win - ning;
Let thy con-gre - ga-tion es - cape ___ trib - u - la - tion.

Sing prais - es to his name; __ he for - gets not his own.
Thou, Lord, wast at our side, __ all __ glo - ry be thine.
Thy name be ev - er praised! _ O __ Lord, make us free!

Do you know what it means to sing "out of tune"? "Out of tune" is a phrase people use to describe a performance that is off pitch. The performers do not sing wrong notes, but they sing a little above or below the notes. This makes the performance sound weak and unpleasant.

You can help yourself to sing "in tune" by finding tricky sections of a song and practicing them.

For example, the descant at the bottom of the page contains some skips that might be tricky to sing in tune. Sing the patterns below. Then sing the descant on "la." Then add the words. Choose the part that best fits the range of your voice. A few will sing the higher part; most may sing the lower part.

La la la la la la    La la la la la la

La la la la la la

*Descant*

We all ex - tol thee, thou lead - er tri - um - phant,

And pray thou still our de - fend - er will be.

Ah _____    Ah _____

Thy __ name be praised! O Lord, make us free!

# God Rest You Merry, Gentlemen

Traditional English Carol
Arranged by Buryl Red

Com-fort and joy!    Com-fort and joy!

Com-fort and joy! _____

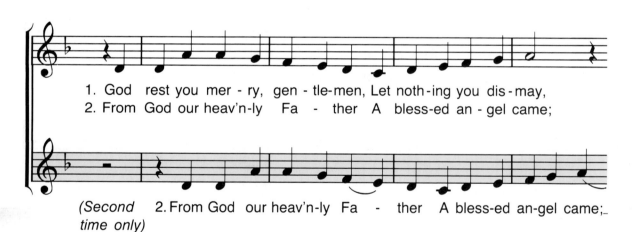

1. God rest you mer - ry, gen - tle-men, Let noth-ing you dis - may,
2. From God our heav'n-ly Fa - ther A bless-ed an - gel came;

(Second    2. From God our heav'n-ly Fa - ther A bless-ed an-gel came;_
time only)

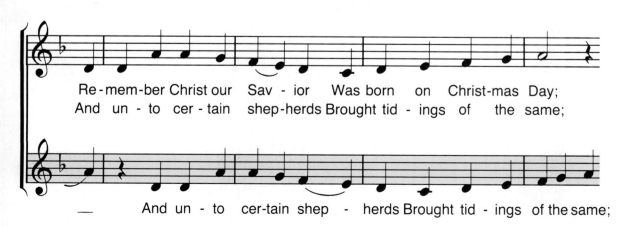

Re - mem-ber Christ our Sav - ior Was born on Christ-mas Day;
And un - to cer - tain shep-herds Brought tid - ings of the same;

— And un - to cer-tain shep - herds Brought tid - ings of the same;

To save us all from Sa-tan's pow'r When we were gone a - stray.
How that in Beth-le - hem was born The Son of God by name.

Ooo _____

O ___ tid - ings of com - fort and joy, com-fort and joy;

*2nd time to Coda* ⊕

3

O ___ tid - ings of com - fort and joy!

⊕ *Coda*

joy! Com-fort and joy! Com-fort and joy! _____

# Fum, Fum, Fum

English Words Adapted

Spanish Carol

mild, Son of Mar - y, Vir - gin Ho - ly, in a

*Fum,       fum,            fum,*

2nd time to ⊕

sta - ble small and    low - ly, *Fum,      fum,        fum.*

*Fum,      fum,          fum, ___ Fum,      fum,        fum.*

On De-cem - ber    five  and twen - ty, *Fum,       fum,        fum,*

On De-cem - ber    five and twen - ty, *Fum,      fum,      fum,*    There was

⊕  *decresc.*                                    *pp*

*Fum,   fum,    fum,      Fum,      fum,        fum. _____*

*Fum,   fum,    fum,      Fum,      fum,        fum. _____*

249

# Pine Cones and Holly Berries

from *Here's Love*

with "It's Beginning to Look Like Christmas"
Words and Music by Meredith Willson

Part 1

Pine    cones    and    hol - ly ber-ries,

Part 2

It's   be - gin-ning to look a lot   like    Christ-mas,

Pop - corn    for    you,      ap - ples    for   me.

Ev  -  ery - where   you     go;        There's a

Red  -  strip - ed can - dy,    nut  -  crack - er han - dy,

tree in the Grand Ho-tel,      One in the park, as well,    The

Ket - tle     a - bub - ble-in'    hol - i - day   tea.

stur - dy kind    that does-n't mind the snow.      It's be -

250

Snow clouds hang low and threat-nin',
gin-ning to look a lot like Christ - mas,
May - be it won't, pray - in' it may. The
Soon the bells will start; And the
bright - est fire - place glows in ev - ery face
thing that will make them ring Is the car - ol that you sing right with -
wait - ing for Christ - mas Day.
in your heart.

# Glossary

**Accent** a sound performed more heavily than other sounds, *24*

**Allegretto** moderately fast, *154*

**Andante** medium speed (a walking tempo), *158*

**Andantino** slightly faster than andante, *176*

**Articulation** how sounds start and stop, *24*

**Bass Clef** or F clef, shows that F below middle C is on the fourth line of the staff, *154*

**Beat** the steady pulse of the music, *53*

**Brass Family** wind instruments made of brass or other metal including the trumpet, French horn, trombone, and tuba, *61*

**Canon** music in which a melody is imitated exactly by another voice or instrument, *91*

**Chord** three or more pitches occurring at the same time, *28*

**Coda** a short concluding section of a piece, *113*

**Countermelody** a second melody placed against the primary melody, *209*

**Descant** a harmony part that is played or sung above the melody, *209*

**Development** the section of a piece in which the main musical material is transformed or expanded, *111*

**Drone** an accompaniment part using only one pitch, *91*

**Dynamics** the loud and soft changes in music, *26*

**Exposition** the section of a piece that presents the main musical material, *110*

**Fermata** (⌒) a note held longer than usual, *110*

**Flat** (♭) a sign that lowers the pitch a half step, *84*

**Form** the design of a piece of music made up of same, similar, or different parts, *122*

**Forte** ( *f* ) loud, *70*

**Fortissimo** ( *ff* ) very loud, *36*

**Fugue** a musical composition in which a main theme is imitated by several voices or instruments entering at different times, *21*

**Harmony** two or more melodies performed at the same time or one melody accompanied by chords, *90*

**Home Tone** scale step 1, also called the *tonal center*, *48*

**Improvisation** creating or composing music as one performs it, without reading musical notation, *53*

**Interval** the distance in pitch between two tones, *93*

**Key Signature** the sharps and flats at the beginning of the music that show where the home tone is located and the kind of scale used, *85*

**Largo** very slow, *188*

**Legato** performed in a smooth, connected way, *65*

**Melody** a series of tones arranged rhythmically to make a musical idea, *122*

**Meter Signature** the two numbers at the beginning of a piece of music that tell how the beats are grouped and show the kind of note that moves with the beat, *44*

**Mezzo Forte** (*mf* ) medium loud, *71*

**Mezzo Piano** (*mp*) medium soft, *37*

**Minuet** a popular dance of the seventeenth and eighteenth centuries, based on a meter signature of $\frac{3}{4}$ and performed at a moderate tempo, *118*

**Moderato** at a moderate speed, *50*

**Movement(s)** the sections of a long composition, *27*

**Musical Comedy** a humorous play containing music, *130*

**Ostinato** an accompaniment pattern repeated over and over, *91*

**Parallel Motion** melodies moving together, always the same distance apart, *94*

**Passing Tone** a tone that moves by whole or half step between two important tones in a chord or scale, *178*

**Percussion Family** instruments played by shaking or by striking, including the drum set, celesta, chimes, orchestra bells, and timpani, *61*

**Pianissimo** (*pp*) very soft, *37*

**Piano** (*p*) soft, *36*

**Pitch** the highness or lowness of a musical sound, *24*

**Polyphony** two or more different melodies heard at the same time, *91*

**Raga** a group of pitches similar to a melody, used in East Indian music as a basis for improvisation, *199*

**Recapitulation** the section of a piece that restates the main musical material, *112*

**Rest** a sign that shows the length of a silence, *10*

**Rhythm** the pattern of long and short sounds and rests, *122*

**Samba** a lively Brazilian dance based on $\frac{2}{4}$ meter and performed at moderate to fast tempos, *77*

**Scat Singing** jazz vocal improvisation using nonsense syllables, *216*

**Sharp** (♯) a sign that raises the pitch a half step, *84*

**Staccato** performed in a short, separated way, *65*

**String Family** instruments played by plucking or bowing strings, including the violin, viola, cello, and double bass, *60*

**Subject** the main melody of a musical composition, *21*

**Suite** a collection of movements, *182*

**Syncopation** a type of rhythm that is created when the accents in a melody occur at a different time from the accented beat, *74*

**Synthesizer** an electronic instrument used to produce and organize musical sounds, *89*

**Tala** a rhythmic pattern or cycle played on percussion instruments in East Indian music, *200*

**Tempo** the speed of the beat, *67*

**Theme** a melody or phrase used as a basic building block for a musical composition, *45*

**Tonal Center** the pitch to which all tones in a piece of music seem to return—the home tone, *48*

**Tone Quality** how the tone sounds, as in rough, sweet, powerful, etc., *193*

**Transpose** to write or perform a melody in a different key, higher or lower, *84*

**Treble Clef** or G clef, shows that G above middle C is on the second line of the staff, *154*

**Triad** a chord that has three pitches: a root, the third, and the fifth, *92*

**Unison** the performance of a single melody by several voices or instruments, *93*

**Variation** a musical idea that is repeated with some change, *45*

**Voice Placement** controlling the quality or color of the voice as one sings, *236*

**Woodwind Family** wind instruments usually made of wood or metal, including the piccolo, flute, oboe, clarinet, and bassoon, *60*

# Acknowledgments

Grateful acknowledgment is made to the following copyright owners and agents for their permission to reprint the following copyrighted material. Every effort has been made to locate all copyright owners; any errors or omissions in copyright notice are inadvertent and will be corrected as they are discovered.

"Ac-cent-tchu-ate the Positive," words by Johnny Mercer, music by Harold Arlen. © 1944 HARWIN MUSIC CO. © Renewed 1972 HARWIN MUSIC CO. International Copyright Secured. All Rights Reserved. Used By Permission of MPL Communications Inc. Recording licensed through the Harry Fox Agency.

"Ama Lama," from *Circle 'Round the Zero* by Maureen Kenney. Copyright © 1983 by Maureen Kenney. Reprinted by permission of MMB Music. Recording licensed through the Harry Fox Agency.

"Are You From Dixie?" words by Jack Yellen, music by George L. Cobb. © 1915 (Renewed) WARNER BROS. INC. All Rights Reserved. Reprinted by Permission. Recording licensed through the Harry Fox Agency.

"As The Sun Goes Down," words and music by Josef Marais (ASCAP). Copyright 1942, 1969, Fideree Music Co. Reprinted and recorded by permission of the publisher.

"Baby's Hi-Fi," words by Frederick Winsor and Marian Parry, from "The Space Child's Mother Goose," by Frederick Winsor and Marian Parry. Simon & Schuster, 1958. Copyright 1958, 1986. Words reprinted and recorded by permission of Margaret Stubbs. Music by Fred Willman, from *Five Spacey Nursery Rhymes,* copyright © 1981 by G. Schirmer. Music reprinted and recorded by permission of Music Sales Corp.

"Beauty," a poem from *I Am a Pueblo Indian Girl* by E-Yeh Shure. Copyright © 1939 by William Morrow & Company, Inc.; renewed 1967 by Louise Abeita Chiwiwi. Reprinted by permission of William Morrow & Company, Inc.

"Bells in the Steeple," translated by Carl Orff, from MUSIC FOR CHILDREN, Vol. 1. © B. Schott's Soehne, Mainz, 1956. © renewed. All Rights Reserved Reprinted by permission of European American Music Distributors Corporation, sole U.S. agent for B. Schott's Soehne. Recording licensed through the Harry Fox Agency.

"Bells of St. Mary's," words by Douglas Furber, music by A. Emmett Adams. Copyright 1917 by Ascherberg, Hopwood & Crew Ltd (London). Copyright Renewed, Chappell & Co., Inc., Publisher for the USA and Canada. International Copyright Secured. ALL RIGHTS RESERVED. Reprinted in the United States and Canada by permission of Hal Leonard Publishing Corporation. Recording licensed through the Harry Fox Agency.

"The Bicycle Song," words and music by Jack Noble White, arranged by Buryl Red. Copyright © 1987 by Kesco Enterprises, Inc. All rights reserved. Reprinted and recorded by permission of the publisher.

"Boogie-Woogie Ghost," by Nadine L. Peglar. Reprinted from INSTRUCTOR, October 1973. Copyright © 1973 by the Instructor Publications, LTD. Reprinted and recorded by permission of the publisher.

"The Cage," by Charles E. Ives, from *114 Songs.* © Copyright 1955 by Peer International Corporation. Copyright Renewed. Reprinted by Permission. Recording licensed through the Harry Fox Agency.

"The City Blues," verses one and three by Jerry Silverman, copyright 1983 by Saw Mill Music Corp. Reprinted and recorded by permission of Saw Mill Music Corp. All rights reserved. Remaining verses by Eugene W. Troth, from *New Dimensions in Music: Experiencing Music* by Robert A. Choate, Lee Kjelson, Richard C. Berg and Eugene W. Troth, copyright © 1970 by Litton Educational Publishing, Inc. Reprinted and recorded by permission of D. C. Heath and Co.

"The Counting Game," by Grant Beglarian. Copyright © 1966 by Grant Beglarian. Reprinted and recorded by permission of the author.

"The Country Party and Old Brass Wagon," medley of "The Monkey's Wedding" and "Old Brass Wagon," from *The Promised Land: A Medley of Pioneer Songs,* arranged by Buryl Red. Copyright © 1976 by Trigon Music, A Division of Triune Music, Inc. Reprinted and recorded by permission of the publisher.

"Dance of the Sugar-Plum Fairy," from *Nutcracker Suite* by Peter I. Tchaikovsky: Arrangement by Frederick Beckman, From *The Magic of Music—Book Six,* © Copyright, 1971, 1968, by Silver, Burdett & Ginn Inc. Reprinted and recorded by permission of the publisher.

"Dixie," words and music by Dan Emmett. © 1961 WARNER BROS. INC. All Rights Reserved. Reprinted by Permission. Recording licensed through the Harry Fox Agency.

"Freedom," words by Julie Barrier, music by Buryl Red, arranged by Buryl Red. Copyright © 1985 Generic Music. All rights reserved. Reprinted and recorded by permission of the publisher.

"Freedom," from *Shenandoah,* lyric by Peter Udell, music by Gary Geld. © 1974, 1975 GARY GELD and PETER UDELL. All Rights Controlled by EDWIN H. MORRIS & COMPANY, A Division of MPL Communications, Inc. International Copyright Secured. All Rights Reserved. Used By Permission. Recording licensed through the Harry Fox Agency.

"Go Down The Wishin' Road," words and music by Blake Alphonso Higgs, Arnold Stanton and Jessie Cavanaugh. TRO—© Copyright 1953 and re-

# Photo Credits

# Art Credits

# Alphabetical Index of Music